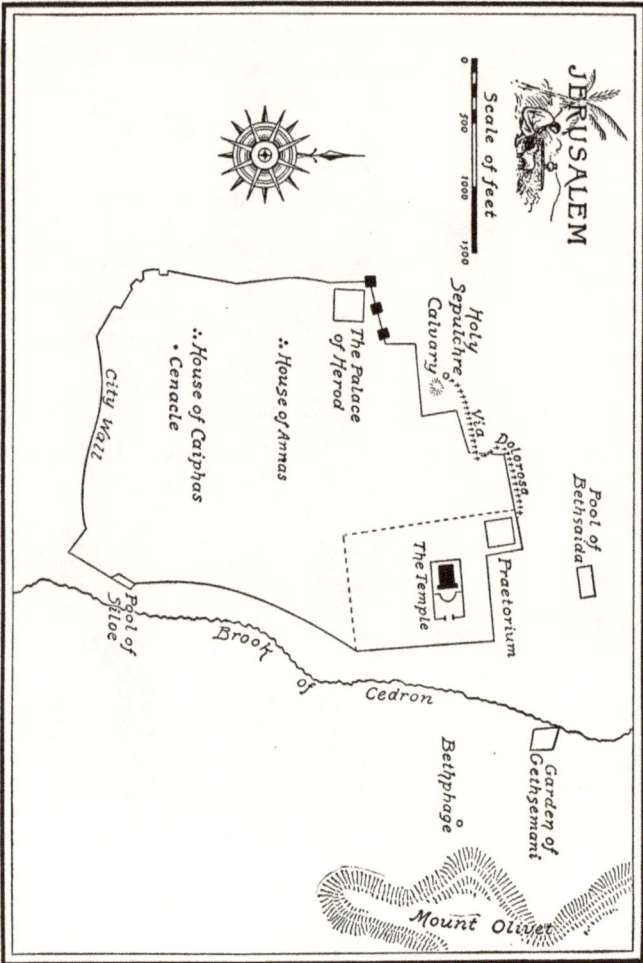

JERUSALEM

Scale of feet
0
500
1000
1500

The Palace of Herod

Holy Sepulchre
Calvary
Via Dolorosa

House of Annas

House of Caiphas
Cenacle

City Wall

Pool of Bethsaida

The Temple
Praetorium

Pool of Siloe

Brook of Cedron

Garden of Gethsemani

Bethphage

Mount Oliver

THE JOURNEYS OF JESUS

COMPILED FROM
THE GOSPEL NARRATIVE

BOOK THREE

SISTER JAMES STANISLAUS
OF THE SISTERS OF ST. JOSEPH OF CARONDELET
ST. LOUIS, MISSOURI

WITH ILLUSTRATIONS AFTER BIDA

ST. AUGUSTINE ACADEMY PRESS
HOMER GLEN, ILLINOIS

𝔑𝔦𝔥𝔦𝔩 ©𝔟𝔰𝔱𝔞𝔱

STI. LUDOVICI, DIE 9 FEBRUARII 1928

JOANNES ROTHENSTEINER
CENSOR LIBRORUM

𝔍𝔪𝔭𝔯𝔦𝔪𝔞𝔱𝔲𝔯

STI. LUDOVICI, DIE 9 FEBRUARII 1928

✠ JOANNES J. GLENNON
ARCHIEPISCOPUS
STI. LUDOVICI

This book was originally published in 1928
by Ginn and Company.

This facsimile edition was reproduced in 2025
by St. Augustine Academy Press.

ISBN: 978-1-64051-134-7

PREFACE

Book Three of "The Journeys of Jesus" is a continuation of the record of events of the Public Ministry of Jesus begun in Book One of the series. The present volume includes the last of the ten Journeys, and relates the incidents that took place during the closing days of Our Lord's Public Ministry.

Each event as narrated in the Gospel during this period forms a distinct topic in one chapter, given in the words of the New Testament. The descriptions of places and buildings at the ends of the chapters have been gathered from reliable sources. At the end of each narrative, questions on the text are included.

Maps and numerous illustrations form an attractive feature of the books and serve to impress and make clearer the lesson of the printed page. A Biblical Glossary of names, with their pronunciations and definitions, is found at the end of the book.

The author wishes to express her deep appreciation and grateful acknowledgment to the B. Herder Book Company for permission to use the classification of places into journeys as given in the "Life of Jesus Christ," by A. J. Maas, of the Society of Jesus.

[v]

CONTENTS

THE END OF THE PUBLIC MINISTRY OF JESUS

THE LAST GREAT JOURNEY

CONTENTS

CONTENTS

[ix]

CONTENTS

CONTENTS

[xi]

THE JOURNEYS OF JESUS

BOOK THREE

THE END
OF THE PUBLIC MINISTRY OF JESUS

JESUS ENTERING JERUSALEM

"And they brought the ass and the colt, and laid their garments upon
them, and made Him sit thereon"

THE LAST GREAT JOURNEY

I

THE ENTRY INTO JERUSALEM

THE TRIUMPH OF JESUS

While Jesus was still in Bethany, the people in Jerusalem were disputing among themselves as to whether or not He would come to the Holy City at this time for the Feast of the Passover. In the midst of the discussion word reached them that Jesus was on His way to Jerusalem.

"And when they drew nigh to Jerusalem, and were come to Bethphage, unto Mount Olivet, then Jesus sent two disciples,

"Saying to them: Go ye into the village that is over against you, and immediately you shall find an ass tied, and a colt with her: loose them and bring them to Me.

"And if any man shall say anything to you, say ye, that the Lord hath need of them: and forthwith he will let them go.

"Now all this was done that it might be fulfilled which was spoken by the prophet, saying:

THE JOURNEYS OF JESUS

"*Tell ye the daughter of Sion: Behold thy king cometh to thee, meek, and sitting upon an ass, and a colt the foal of her that is used to the yoke.*

"And the disciples going, did as Jesus commanded them.

"And they brought the ass and the colt, and laid their garments upon them, and made Him sit thereon.

"And a very great multitude spread their garments in the way: and others cut boughs from the trees, and strewed them in the way:

"And the multitudes that went before and that followed, cried, saying: *Hosanna to the Son of David: Blessed is He that cometh in the Name of the Lord: Hosanna in the highest.*

"And when He was come into Jerusalem, the whole city was moved, saying: Who is this?

"And the people said: This is Jesus the Prophet, from Nazareth of Galilee." (St. Matthew xxi, 1–11.)

BETHPHAGE

Bethphage, meaning the House of Green Figs, was a little village near Jerusalem. It was to the right of travelers going toward Jerusalem from Bethany. The stony fields on either side of the road were planted with fig trees and surrounded by vineyards bearing a plentiful harvest of rich fruit.

[6]

THE ENTRY INTO JERUSALEM

QUESTIONS

1. When Jesus entered Jerusalem, He was not at the head of the line of march. How did this happen?

2. Quote the people's words of greeting to Jesus on His entrance into Jerusalem.

3. What actions showed that the people regarded Jesus as the promised Messias?

4. Why did not the chief priests and Scribes join in honoring Jesus?

5. Why are palms blessed?

6. Why are blessed palms carried in the hand during the reading of the Gospel on Palm Sunday?

7. Show on the map about where Bethphage was.

JESUS WEEPS OVER JERUSALEM

The Pharisees were very much disturbed by this homage given to Our Saviour. They thought that Jesus should not accept such a public tribute, and some of them said to Him: "Master, rebuke Thy disciples." They meant "Tell Thy followers not to exalt Thee so much."

Whereupon Jesus said to them: "I say to you, that if these shall hold their peace, the stones will cry out."

In the midst of all this triumph, Jesus was sad. He was thinking of how this same city, which now seemed wild with joy to see Him, would in a few

JESUS WEEPETH OVER JERUSALEM

days reject Him: and He foresaw the ruin of the city because of this rejection. Therefore "when He drew near, seeing the city, He wept over it, saying:

"If thou also hadst known, and that in this thy day, the things that are to thy peace; but now they are hidden from thy eyes.

"For the days shall come upon thee: and thy enemies shall cast a trench about thee, and compass thee round, and straiten thee on every side,

"And beat thee flat to the ground, and thy children who are in thee: and they shall not leave in thee a stone upon a stone: because thou hast not known the time of thy visitation." (St. Luke xix, 39–44.)

After this day of triumph, Jesus, surrounded by His disciples, went in the direction of Bethania, where He was to spend the night.

QUESTIONS

1. What prophecy concerning Jerusalem did Jesus make "when He drew near, seeing the city"?

2. Where in the Bible can this prophecy be found?

II

ON THE WAY FROM BETHANIA

The Barren Fig Tree

Jesus and His Apostles had left the multitude and had spent the night at Bethania. St. Mark relates an incident which took place at this time.

"And the next day when they came out from Bethania, He was hungry.

"And when He had seen afar off a fig tree having leaves, He came if perhaps He might find any thing on it. And when He was come to it, He found nothing but leaves. For it was not the time for figs.

"And answering He said to it: May no man hereafter eat fruit of thee any more for ever. And His disciples heard it." (St. Mark xi, 12–14.)

Pliny in his "Historia Naturalis," chap. xvi, p. 49, says "the fig tree had a rich foliage, which was a sign of an early crop." This tree puts forth its fruit before it is well leaved out. Although it was not now the time for figs, the abundant growth of leaves gave promise of an early crop of fruit. Finding the leaves a false promise, Our Lord cursed the tree.

III

IN THE TEMPLE

THE SECOND PURIFICATION OF THE TEMPLE

Although it was an early hour when Jesus and His disciples reached the Temple, the courts were crowded with those engaged in buying and selling beasts for the sacrifices. On a former occasion Our Lord had driven out those who disgraced the House of God by their traffic. Now His eyes beheld the Temple again profaned by these men, and again His indignation was great.

"And Jesus went into the Temple of God, and cast out all them that sold and bought in the Temple, and overthrew the tables of the money changers, and the chairs of them that sold doves:

"And He saith to them: It is written, *My house shall be called the house of prayer; but you have made it a den of thieves.*

"And there came to Him the blind and the lame in the Temple; and He healed them.

"And the chief priests and Scribes, seeing the wonderful things that He did, and the children cry-

THE TEMPLE

ing in the Temple, and saying: *Hosanna to the Son of David*; were moved with indignation,

"And said to Him: Hearest Thou what these say? And Jesus said to them: Yea, have you never read: *Out of the mouth of infants and of sucklings thou hast perfected praise?*" (St. Matthew xxi, 12–16.)

QUESTIONS

1. How did Jesus show His authority on Monday morning of this Holy Week?

2. Is there such a thing as just anger?

3. Give an example of an incident in which anger is not a sin.

4. Read the account of the First Purification of the Temple. When did it take place? (See Book One of "The Journeys of Jesus.")

IV

OUTSIDE THE TEMPLE

"Now there were certain Gentiles among them, who came up to adore on the festival day.

"These therefore came to Philip, who was of Bethsaida of Galilee, and desired him, saying: Sir, we would see Jesus.

"Philip cometh, and telleth Andrew. Again Andrew and Philip told Jesus.

"But Jesus answered them, saying: The hour is come, that the Son of Man should be glorified.

"Amen, amen I say to you, unless the grain of wheat falling into the ground die,

"Itself remaineth alone. But if it die, it bringeth forth much fruit. He that loveth his life shall lose it; and he that hateth his life in this world, keepeth it unto life eternal.

"If any man minister to Me, let him follow Me; and where I am, there also shall My minister be. If any man minister to Me, him will My Father honor.

"Now is My soul troubled. And what shall I say?

[14]

Father, save Me from this hour. But for this cause I came unto this hour.

"Father, glorify Thy Name. A Voice therefore came from heaven: I have both glorified It, and will glorify It again.

"The multitude therefore that stood and heard, said that it thundered. Others said: An angel spoke to Him.

"Jesus answered, and said: This Voice came not because of Me, but for your sakes.

"Now is the judgment of the world: now shall the prince of this world be cast out.

"And I, if I be lifted up from the earth, will draw all things to Myself.

"(Now this He said, signifying what death He should die.)

"The multitude answered Him: We have heard out of the Law, that Christ abideth for ever; and how sayest Thou: The Son of Man must be lifted up? Who is this Son of Man?

"Jesus therefore said to them: Yet a little while, the Light is among you. Walk whilst you have the Light, that the darkness overtake you not. And he that walketh in darkness, knoweth not whither he goeth.

"Whilst you have the Light, believe in the Light, that you may be the children of light. These things

Jesus spoke; and He went away, and hid Himself from them." (St. John xii, 20–36.)

Our Lord's reply to the Jews made it clear to them that He, Himself, is the Light of the World, but the Jews did not, or would not, understand. And even those who did believe were afraid to express their belief in Christ. They did not confess Him for fear they might be cast out of the synagogues. "For," says St. John, "they loved the glory of men more than the glory of God." (St. John xii, 43.)

QUESTIONS

1. How did it happen that Gentiles were present in the Temple at this time?

2. Upon what occasion did Jesus utter these words: "Unless the grain of wheat falling into the ground die, itself remaineth alone. But if it die, it bringeth forth much fruit"?

3. In what words did Jesus predict the manner of His death on a Cross?

4. What is the meaning of the words, "I, if I be lifted up from the earth, will draw all things to Myself"?

5. Find in Book Two of "The Journeys of Jesus" the occasion upon which Our Lord said, "When I am lifted up."

6. Tell what these words mean: "Yet a little while, the Light is among you."

OUTSIDE THE TEMPLE

THE FIG TREE BLASTED

The day following, Jesus and the Apostles passed by the fig tree which He had cursed the day before. Now it was parched, and withered to the root.

"And Peter remembering, said to Him: Rabbi, behold the fig tree, which Thou didst curse, is withered away.

"And Jesus answering, saith to them: Have the faith of God.

"Amen I say to you, that whosoever shall say to this mountain, Be thou removed and be cast into the sea, and shall not stagger in his heart, but believe, that whatsoever he saith shall be done; it shall be done unto him.

"Therefore I say unto you, all things, whatsoever you ask when ye pray, believe that you shall receive; and they shall come unto you.

"And when you shall stand to pray, forgive, if you have aught against any man; that your Father also, Who is in heaven, may forgive you your sins." (St. Mark xi, 20–25.)

QUESTIONS

1. Why did Christ curse the fig tree?

2. When Peter called the attention of Jesus to the withered tree, what did Jesus say about prayer and faith?

V

IN THE HOLY CITY

The Beginning of the Final Conflict

Coming again to the Temple, Jesus was approached by the chief priests, the Scribes, and the ancients.

"And they say to Him: By what authority dost Thou these things? and who hath given Thee this authority that Thou shouldst do these things?

"And Jesus answering, said to them: I will also ask you one word, and answer you Me, and I will tell you by what authority I do these things.

"The baptism of John, was it from heaven, or from men? Answer Me.

"But they thought with themselves, saying: If we say, From heaven; He will say, Why then did you not believe him?

"If we say, From men, we fear the people. For all men counted John that he was a prophet indeed.

"And they answering, say to Jesus: We know not. And Jesus answering, saith to them: Neither do I tell you by what authority I do these things." (St. Mark xi, 28–33.)

[18]

IN THE HOLY CITY

QUESTIONS

1. Why did the chief priests and Scribes not answer the question Jesus put to them?

2. Where did this conversation take place?

The Parable of the Wicked Husbandmen

"And He began to speak to them in parables: A certain man planted a vineyard and made a hedge about it, and dug a place for the winefat, and built a tower, and let it to husbandmen; and went into a far country.

"And at the season he sent to the husbandmen a servant to receive of the husbandmen of the fruit of the vineyard.

"Who having laid hands on him, beat him, and sent him away empty.

"And again he sent to them another servant; and him they wounded in the head, and used him reproachfully.

"And again he sent another, and him they killed: and many others, of whom some they beat, and others they killed.

"Therefore having yet one son, most dear to him; he also sent him unto them last of all, saying: They will reverence my son.

"But the husbandmen said one to another: This

is the heir; come let us kill him; and the inheritance shall be ours.

"And laying hold on him, they killed him, and cast him out of the vineyard.

"What therefore will the lord of the vineyard do? He will come and destroy those husbandmen; and will give the vineyard to others.

"And have you not read this Scripture, *The stone which the builders rejected, the same is made the head of the corner:*

"*By the Lord has this been done, and it is wonderful in our eyes.*

"And they sought to lay hands on Him, but they feared the people. For they knew that He spoke this parable to them. And leaving Him, they went their way." (St. Mark xii, 1–12.)

QUESTIONS

1. Whom do you think Our Lord meant by the Father Who sent His Son to the husbandmen to receive the fruit of the vineyard?

2. Do you think the Pharisees knew that Jesus meant them when He said that the Lord of the vineyard would come and destroy the husbandmen?

3. Why did they fear to lay hands on Jesus?

4. Can you tell why Our Lord so frequently used the vineyard as a symbol in His parables?

IN THE HOLY CITY

THE PARABLE OF THE MARRIAGE FEAST

"And Jesus answering, spoke again in parables to them, saying:

"The Kingdom of Heaven is likened to a king, who made a marriage for his son.

"And he sent his servants, to call them that were invited to the marriage; and they would not come.

"Again he sent other servants, saying: Tell them that were invited, Behold, I have prepared my dinner; my beeves and fatlings are killed, and all things are ready: come ye to the marriage.

"But they neglected, and went their ways, one to his farm, and another to his merchandise.

"And the rest laid hands on his servants, and having treated them contumeliously, put them to death.

"But when the king had heard of it, he was angry, and sending his armies, he destroyed those murderers, and burnt their city.

"Then he saith to his servants: The marriage indeed is ready; but they that were invited were not worthy.

"Go ye therefore into the highways; and as many as you shall find, call to the marriage.

"And his servants going forth into the ways, gathered together all that they found, both bad and good: and the marriage was filled with guests.

THE JOURNEYS OF JESUS

"And the king went in to see the guests: and he saw there a man who had not on a wedding garment.

"And he saith to him: Friend, how camest thou in hither not having on a wedding garment? But he was silent.

"Then the king said to the waiters: Bind his hands and feet, and cast him into the exterior darkness: there shall be weeping and gnashing of teeth.

"For many are called, but few are chosen." (St. Matthew xxii, 1–14.)

QUESTIONS

1. What do you understand by the wedding garment mentioned in this parable?

2. Give the words of the parable that indicate the call of the Gentiles.

3. Give the words that foretell the destruction of Jerusalem.

4. In what way have these words been fulfilled?

To Cæsar the Things that are Cæsar's

The Herodians were members of a political body of Jews, whose special aim was to promote Herod's interests, and who in consequence acknowledged the Roman laws and rules. The Pharisees and Sadducees talked together privately with the Herodians and

CÆSAR'S PENNY

agreed to propose to Jesus three questions, hoping to find in His answers something against the Law of Moses or against the Roman government. The first question concerned the tribute money.

They said to Jesus: "Master, we know that Thou art a true speaker, and teachest the way of God in truth, neither carest Thou for any man: for Thou dost not regard the person of men.

"Tell us therefore what dost Thou think, is it lawful to give tribute to Cæsar, or not?

"But Jesus knowing their wickedness, said: Why do you tempt Me, ye hypocrites?

"Show Me the coin of the tribute. And they offered Him a penny.

"And Jesus saith to them: Whose image and inscription is this?

"They say to Him: Cæsar's. Then He saith to them: Render therefore to Cæsar the things that are Cæsar's; and to God, the things that are God's.

"And hearing this they wondered, and leaving Him, went their ways." (St. Matthew xxii, 16–22.)

The Wife of Seven Brothers

"That day there came to Him the Sadducees, who say there is no resurrection; and asked Him,

"Saying: Master, Moses said: *If a man die hav-*

ing no son, his brother shall marry his wife, and raise up issue to his brother.

"Now there were with us seven brethren: and the first having married a wife, died; and not having issue, left his wife to his brother.

"In like manner the second, and the third, and so on to the seventh.

"And last of all the woman died also.

"At the resurrection therefore whose wife of the seven shall she be? for they all had her.

"And Jesus answering, said to them: You err, not knowing the Scriptures, nor the power of God.

"For in the resurrection they shall neither marry nor be married; but shall be as the angels of God in heaven.

"And concerning the resurrection of the dead, have you not read that which was spoken by God, saying to you:

"*I am the God of Abraham, and the God of Isaac, and the God of Jacob?* He is not the God of the dead, but of the living.

"And the multitudes hearing it, were in admiration at His Doctrine." (St. Matthew xxii, 23–33.)

QUESTIONS

1. Who were the Sadducees?
2. In what article of our faith did they not believe?

[25]

THE JOURNEYS OF JESUS

THE PHARISEES SILENCED

Then the Pharisees came to Him, "And one of them, a doctor of the Law, asked Him, tempting Him:

"Master, which is the great commandment in the Law?

"Jesus said to him: *Thou shalt love the Lord thy God with thy whole heart, and with thy whole soul, and with thy whole mind.*

"This is the greatest and the first commandment.

"And the second is like to this: *Thou shalt love thy neighbor as thyself.*

"On these two commandments dependeth the whole Law and the prophets.

"And the Pharisees being gathered together, Jesus asked them,

"Saying: What think you of Christ? Whose Son is He? They say to Him: David's.

"He saith to them: How then doth David in spirit call Him Lord, saying:

"*The Lord said to my Lord, Sit on My right hand, until I make Thy enemies Thy footstool?*

"If David then call Him Lord, how is He his son?

"And no man was able to answer Him a word; neither durst any man from that day forth ask Him any more questions." (St. Matthew xxii, 35–46.)

[26]

"THOU SHALT LOVE THE LORD THY GOD WITH THY
WHOLE HEART"

THE JOURNEYS OF JESUS

QUESTIONS

1. What three classes of people tried to ensnare Jesus on Tuesday of Holy Week?

2. What means did each class use for this purpose?

3. What answer did Christ give about the coin of tribute?

4. What does the Fourth Commandment of God tell us to do about the laws of the country?

5. Is not the law of the country included in the Law of God?

6. Which is the greatest commandment of the Law?

7. Which other is like it?

8. Read in St. Mark xii, 28–34, about the scribe who asked which was the first commandment of all.

THE CHAIR OF MOSES

Jesus thereupon took occasion to rebuke the obstinate pride and hypocrisy of the Pharisees. Speaking to the people and to His disciples, Our Lord said: "The Scribes and the Pharisees have sitten on the chair of Moses.

"All things therefore whatsoever they shall say to you, observe and do: but according to their works do ye not; for they say, and do not.

"For they bind heavy and insupportable burdens, and lay them on men's shoulders; but with a finger of their own they will not move them.

[28]

IN THE HOLY CITY

"And all their works they do for to be seen of men. For they make their phylacteries broad, and enlarge their fringes.

"And they love the first places at feasts, and the first chairs in the synagogues,

"And salutations in the market place, and to be called by men, Rabbi.

"But be not you called Rabbi. For One is your Master; and all you are brethren.

"And call none your father upon earth; for One is your Father, Who is in heaven.

"Neither be ye called masters; for One is your Master, Christ.

"He that is the greatest among you shall be your servant.

"And whosoever shall exalt himself shall be humbled: and he that shall humble himself shall be exalted." (St. Matthew xxiii, 1–12.)

QUESTIONS

1. Give in your own words the meaning of the following: "He that shall humble himself shall be exalted."

2. Name several occasions upon which Christ proved by example the truth of these words of His: "He that is the greatest among you shall be your servant."

THE JOURNEYS OF JESUS

THE DENUNCIATION OF THE PHARISEES

Then Jesus began to utter terrible "woes," saying:
"But woe to you Scribes and Pharisees, hypocrites;
because you shut the Kingdom of Heaven against
men, for you yourselves do not enter in; and those
that are going in, you suffer not to enter.

"Woe to you Scribes and Pharisees, hypocrites;
because you devour the houses of widows, praying
long prayers. For this you shall receive the greater
judgment.

"Woe to you Scribes and Pharisees, hypocrites;
because you go round about the sea and the land to
make one proselyte; and when he is made, you make
him the child of hell twofold more than yourselves.

"Woe to you blind guides, that say, Whosoever
shall swear by the Temple, it is nothing; but he that
shall swear by the gold of the Temple, is a debtor.

"Ye foolish and blind; for whether is greater, the
gold, or the Temple that sanctifieth the gold?

"And whosoever shall swear by the altar, it is
nothing; but whosoever shall swear by the gift that
is upon it, is a debtor.

"Ye blind: for whether is greater, the gift, or the
altar that sanctifieth the gift?

"He therefore that sweareth by the altar, sweareth
by it, and by all things that are upon it:

"And whosoever shall swear by the Temple, sweareth by it, and by Him that dwelleth in it:

"And he that sweareth by heaven, sweareth by the throne of God, and by Him that sitteth thereon.

"Woe to you Scribes and Pharisees, hypocrites; because you tithe mint, and anise, and cummin, and have left the weightier things of the law; judgment, and mercy, and faith. These things you ought to have done, and not to leave those undone.

"Blind guides, who strain out a gnat, and swallow a camel.

"Woe to you Scribes and Pharisees, hypocrites; because you make clean the outside of the cup and of the dish, but within you are full of rapine and uncleanness.

"Thou blind Pharisee, first make clean the inside of the cup and of the dish, that the outside may become clean.

"Woe to you Scribes and Pharisees, hypocrites; because you are like to whited sepulchres, which outwardly appear to men beautiful, but within are full of dead men's bones, and of all filthiness.

"So you also outwardly indeed appear to men just; but inwardly you are full of hypocrisy and iniquity.

"Woe to you Scribes and Pharisees, hypocrites;

that build the sepulchres of the prophets, and adorn the monuments of the just,

"And say: If we had been in the days of our Fathers, we would not have been partakers with them in the blood of the prophets.

"Wherefore you are witnesses against yourselves, that you are the sons of them that killed the prophets.

"Fill ye up then the measure of your fathers." (St. Matthew xxiii, 13–32.)

QUESTIONS

1. Give some of the reasons why Christ denounced the Pharisees.

2. Give the meaning of these words: "First make clean the inside of the cup and of the dish, that the outside may become clean."

3. In what way do you explain the "whited sepulchres" mentioned on this occasion?

4. God judges the inner dispositions. Does it follow that we need not pay any attention to our outward conduct?

5. Find the answer to the fourth question in the Sermon on the Mount. (See St. Matthew v, 16.)

THE LAST PUBLIC DISCOURSE

Jesus, continuing His discourse, foretold the sufferings and persecutions which the Apostles would have to undergo before the destruction of Jerusalem.

He said: "Therefore behold I send to you prophets, and wise men, and scribes: and some of them you will put to death and crucify, and some you will scourge in your synagogues, and persecute from city to city:

"That upon you may come all the just blood that hath been shed upon the earth, from the blood of Abel the just, even unto the blood of Zacharias the son of Barachias, whom you killed between the Temple and the altar.

"Amen I say to you, all these things shall come upon this generation."

Then our Blessed Lord grieved over the Holy City, saying:

"Jerusalem, Jerusalem, thou that killest the prophets, and stonest them that are sent unto thee, how often would I have gathered together thy children, as the hen doth gather her chickens under her wings, and thou wouldest not?

"Behold, your house shall be left to you, desolate.

"For I say to you, you shall not see Me henceforth till you say: Blessed is He that cometh in the Name of the Lord." (St. Matthew xxiii, 34–39.)

This is the last discourse that Jesus addressed to the multitudes. His public teaching, though not His public ministry of healing and of divine example, had come to an end; after this He spoke only to a few chosen disciples, and to them in private.

THE JOURNEYS OF JESUS

QUESTIONS

1. In this last public discourse, to what did Christ liken Himself?

2. Were any of the Saviour's words on this occasion a prophecy to the Apostles?

3. Tell in what way each of the Apostles met death.

VI

NEAR THE HALL OF THE TREASURY

The Widow's Mites

At the end of these discourses Jesus seated Himself apart, in the court of Israel near the hall of the treasury, facing the collection boxes placed to receive the offerings, which were used in the purchase of beasts for the sacrifices.

Jesus looked upon the crowd which thronged about the boxes to throw in their money. The rich, of whom there were many, threw in large sums, and the people watched them and marveled at them. But among them a poor widow stole up to the box and dropped in her treasure—"two mites, which make a farthing."

And Jesus, seeing this, called His disciples and pointed out this humble soul to them, saying: "Amen I say to you, this poor widow hath cast in more than all they who have cast into the treasury.

"For all they did cast in of their abundance; but she of her want cast in all she had, even her whole living." (St. Mark xii, 41–44.)

THE WIDOW'S MITES

NEAR THE HALL OF THE TREASURY

QUESTION

"The rich . . . threw in large sums." In what sense did Jesus mean that the widow had "cast in more than all they," since she had dropped into the treasury only "two mites, which make a farthing"?

THE PROPHECY CONCERNING THE TEMPLE

Jesus rose from His seat near the treasury and walked the length of the porches. His disciples following after Him were admiring the splendors of the Temple. Everything about it enchanted their delighted eyes: mosaics, sculptures, colonnades, gateways,—all adorned with precious metals.

It is said that the Temple was built of white marble exquisitely carved. Some of the stones were fifty feet long, sixteen feet high, and twenty-four feet thick. On every side they were covered with solid plates of gold, and when the sun rose and cast its rays upon the roof the reflection was so strong and dazzling that the eye could not endure its radiance.

The Apostles' admiration for the building was so great that, going out of the Temple, one of them said to Jesus: "Master, behold what manner of stones, and what buildings are here."

Jesus replied: "Seest thou all these great buildings? There shall not be left a stone upon a stone, that shall not be thrown down." Such was the Saviour's farewell to the Temple. (St. Mark xiii, 1–2.)

QUESTIONS

1. Find out how long after Jesus foretold the destruction of the Temple the event actually happened.

2. Can you tell something about the destruction of Jerusalem?

3. Has the city ever been rebuilt with the same magnificence as in the days of Christ?

VII

ON MOUNT OLIVET

The Signs of the Lord's Coming

The little company then left the Temple, crossed the Cedron Brook or Gorge, and climbed up the slopes of the Mount of Olives. When they had reached the summit, Jesus sat down and silently faced the Temple, gazing upon the city which He was never again to enter, except to die.

"And when He was sitting on Mount Olivet, the disciples came to Him privately, saying: Tell us when shall these things be? and what shall be the sign of Thy coming, and of the consummation of the world?

"And Jesus answering, said to them: Take heed that no man seduce you:

"For many will come in My Name saying, I am Christ: and they will seduce many.

"And you shall hear of wars and rumors of wars. See that ye be not troubled. For these things must come to pass, but the end is not yet.

"For nation shall rise against nation, and kingdom

against kingdom; and there shall be pestilences, and famines, and earthquakes in places:

"Now all these are the beginnings of sorrows.

"Then shall they deliver you up to be afflicted, and shall put you to death: and you shall be hated by all nations for My Name's sake.

"And then shall many be scandalized: and shall betray one another: and shall hate one another.

"And many false prophets shall rise, and shall seduce many.

"And because iniquity hath abounded, the charity of many shall grow cold.

"But he that shall persevere to the end, he shall be saved.

"And this Gospel of the Kingdom, shall be preached in the whole world, for a testimony to all nations, and then shall the consummation come.

"When therefore you shall see the abomination of desolation, which was spoken of by Daniel the prophet, standing in the holy place: he that readeth let him understand.

"Then they that are in Judea, let them flee to the mountains:

"And he that is on the housetop, let him not come down to take any thing out of his house:

"And he that is in the field, let him not go back to take his coat.

JESUS ON THE MOUNT OF OLIVES

"And woe to them that are with child, and that give suck in those days.

"But pray that your flight be not in the winter, or on the Sabbath.

"For there shall be then great tribulation, such as hath not been from the beginning of the world until now, neither shall be.

"And unless those days had been shortened, no flesh should be saved: but for the sake of the elect those days shall be shortened." (St. Matthew xxiv, 3–22.)

QUESTIONS

1. Name some of the signs of the Lord's coming.

2. What part of the Apostles' question did Jesus not answer?

3. Some of these prophecies concerned events which were to happen in the lifetime of the Apostles. Can you tell which these were?

FALSE PROPHETS

"Then if any man shall say to you: Lo here is Christ, or there, do not believe him.

"For there shall arise false Christs and false prophets, and shall show great signs and wonders, insomuch as to deceive (if possible) even the elect.

"Behold I have told it to you, beforehand.

"If therefore they shall say to you: Behold He is

in the desert, go ye not out: Behold He is in the closets, believe it not.

"For as lightning cometh out of the east, and appeareth even into the west: so shall also the coming of the Son of Man be.

"Wheresoever the body shall be, there shall the eagles also be gathered together." (St. Matthew xxiv, 23–28.)

QUESTIONS

1. Can you give the meaning of the word "magician"?

2. Find an account of a famous magician who lived in the time of the Apostles, and relate his deeds to the class.

THE SIGNS IN THE HEAVENS

"And immediately after the tribulation of those days, the sun shall be darkened and the moon shall not give her light, and the stars shall fall from heaven, and the powers of heaven shall be moved:

"And then shall appear the sign of the Son of Man in heaven: and then shall all tribes of the earth mourn: and they shall see the Son of Man coming in the clouds of heaven with much power and majesty.

"And He shall send His angels with a trumpet, and a great voice: and they shall gather together His elect from the four winds, from the farthest parts of the heavens to the utmost bounds of them.

THE JOURNEYS OF JESUS

"And from the fig tree learn a parable: When the branch thereof is now tender, and the leaves come forth, you know that summer is nigh.

"So you also, when you shall see all these things, know ye that it is nigh, even at the doors.

"Amen I say to you, that this generation shall not pass, till all these things be done.

"Heaven and earth shall pass, but My words shall not pass." (St. Matthew xxiv, 29–35.)

QUESTIONS

1. What do you think is the meaning of "the sign of the Son of Man in heaven"?

2. What will be the work of the angels at the second coming of Christ?

3. Quote the words of Jesus that answer the second question.

The Second Coming of Christ

"But of that day and hour no one knoweth, no not the angels of heaven, but the Father alone.

"And as in the days of Noe, so shall also the coming of the Son of Man be.

"For as in the days before the flood, they were eating and drinking, marrying and giving in marriage, even till that day in which Noe entered into the ark,

"And they knew not till the flood came, and took them all away; so also shall the coming of the Son of Man be.

"Then two shall be in the field: one shall be taken, and one shall be left.

"Two women shall be grinding at the mill: one shall be taken, and one shall be left.

"Watch ye therefore, because you know not what hour your Lord will come.

"But this know ye, that if the goodman of the house knew at what hour the thief would come, he would certainly watch, and would not suffer his house to be broken open.

"Wherefore be you also ready, because at what hour you know not the Son of Man will come.

"Who, thinkest thou, is a faithful and wise servant, whom his lord hath appointed over his family, to give them meat in season.

"Blessed is that servant, whom when his lord shall come he shall find so doing.

"Amen I say to you, he shall place him over all his goods.

"But if that evil servant shall say in his heart: My lord is long a coming:

"And shall begin to strike his fellow servants, and shall eat and drink with drunkards:

"The lord of that servant shall come in a day

that he hopeth not, and at an hour that he knoweth not:

"And shall separate him, and appoint his portion with the hypocrites. There shall be weeping and gnashing of teeth." (St. Matthew xxiv, 36–51.)

QUESTIONS

1. Who knows when the end of the world will come?

2. Can you think of a reason why God conceals from us the hour of our death?

3. What meaning do you give to these words: "Watch ye therefore, because you know not what hour your Lord will come"?

4. What have you read about Noe?

5. Can you tell why Christ on this occasion referred to the flood?

The Parable of the Ten Virgins

"Then shall the Kingdom of Heaven be like to ten virgins, who taking their lamps went out to meet the bridegroom and the bride.

"And five of them were foolish, and five wise.

"But the five foolish, having taken their lamps, did not take oil with them:

"But the wise took oil in their vessels with the lamps.

THE FOOLISH VIRGINS

"And the bridegroom tarrying, they all slumbered and slept.

"And at midnight there was a cry made: Behold the bridegroom cometh, go ye forth to meet him.

"Then all those virgins arose and trimmed their lamps.

"And the foolish said to the wise: Give us of your oil, for our lamps are gone out.

"The wise answered, saying: Lest perhaps there be not enough for us and for you, go ye rather to them that sell, and buy for yourselves.

"Now whilst they went to buy, the bridegroom came: and they that were ready, went in with him to the marriage, and the door was shut.

"But at last came also the other virgins, saying: Lord, Lord, open to us.

"But he answering said: Amen I say to you, I know you not.

"Watch ye therefore, because you know not the day nor the hour." (St. Matthew xxv, 1–13.)

QUESTIONS

1. In this parable, do you think that "oil" could mean good works?

2. Will the good works and prayers of others save our souls?

3. Give in your own words the meaning of this parable.

ON MOUNT OLIVET

The Parable of the Faithful and the Unfaithful Servants

Our Lord then repeated a parable which He had related once before: "For even as a man going into a far country, called his servants, and delivered to them his goods;

"And to one he gave five talents, and to another two, and to another one, to every one according to his proper ability: and immediately he took his journey.

"And he that had received the five talents, went his way, and traded with the same, and gained other five.

"And in like manner he that had received the two, gained other two.

"But he that had received the one, going his way digged into the earth, and hid his lord's money.

"But after a long time the lord of those servants came, and reckoned with them.

"And he that had received the five talents coming, brought other five talents, saying: Lord, thou didst deliver to me five talents, behold I have gained other five over and above.

"His lord said to him: Well done, good and faithful servant, because thou hast been faithful over a few things, I will place thee over many things: enter thou into the joy of thy lord.

[49]

"And he also that had received the two talents came and said: Lord, thou deliveredst two talents to me: behold I have gained other two.

"His lord said to him: Well done, good and faithful servant: because thou hast been faithful over a few things, I will place thee over many things: enter thou into the joy of thy lord.

"But he that had received the one talent, came and said: Lord, I know that thou art a hard man; thou reapest where thou hast not sown, and gatherest where thou hast not strewed.

"And being afraid I went and hid thy talent in the earth: behold here thou hast that which is thine.

"And his lord answering, said to him: Wicked and slothful servant, thou knewest that I reap where I sow not, and gather where I have not strewed:

"Thou oughtest therefore to have committed my money to the bankers, and at my coming I should have received my own with usury.

"Take ye away therefore the talent from him, and give it him that hath ten talents.

"For to every one that hath shall be given, and he shall abound: but from him that hath not, that also which he seemeth to have shall be taken away.

"And the unprofitable servant cast ye out into the exterior darkness. There shall be weeping and gnashing of teeth." (St. Matthew xxv, 14–30.)

ON MOUNT OLIVET

QUESTIONS

1. Does Christ require equal service from all men?

2. Does He give the same graces to all men?

3. Besides being a unit of money, what other meaning has the word "talent"?

4. What is the meaning of these words: "Cast ye out into the exterior darkness"?

5. Where shall there be "weeping and gnashing of teeth"?

The Day of the Last Judgment

"And when the Son of Man shall come in His majesty, and all the angels with Him, then shall He sit upon the seat of His majesty:

"And all nations shall be gathered together before Him, and He shall separate them one from another, as the shepherd separateth the sheep from the goats:

"And He shall set the sheep on His right hand, but the goats on His left.

"Then shall the King say to them that shall be on His right hand: Come, ye blessed of My Father, possess you the Kingdom prepared for you from the foundation of the world.

"For I was hungry, and you gave Me to eat; I was thirsty, and you gave Me to drink; I was a stranger, and you took Me in:

"Naked, and you covered Me: sick, and you visited Me: I was in prison, and you came to Me.

"Then shall the just answer Him, saying: Lord, when did we see Thee hungry, and fed Thee; thirsty, and gave Thee drink?

"And when did we see Thee a stranger, and took Thee in? or naked, and covered Thee?

"Or when did we see Thee sick or in prison, and came to Thee?

"And the King answering, shall say to them: Amen I say to you, as long as you did it to one of these My least brethren, you did it to Me.

"Then He shall say to them also that shall be on His left hand: Depart from Me, you cursed, into everlasting fire which was prepared for the devil and his angels.

"For I was hungry, and you gave Me not to eat: I was thirsty, and you gave Me not to drink.

"I was a stranger, and you took Me not in: naked, and you covered Me not: sick and in prison, and you did not visit Me.

"Then they also shall answer Him, saying: Lord, when did we see Thee hungry, or thirsty, or a stranger, or naked, or sick, or in prison, and did not minister to Thee?

"Then He shall answer them, saying: Amen I say

to you, as long as you did it not to one of these least, neither did you do it to Me.

"And these shall go into everlasting punishment: but the just, into life everlasting." (St. Matthew xxv, 31–46.)

QUESTIONS

1. In what way can we provide food, clothing, and shelter for Our Saviour, since He is no longer in need of such things?

2. When is the Last Judgment to take place?

3. Is there another judgment besides this general judgment?

4. To whom do these words of Our Lord apply: "As long as you did it to one of these My least brethren, you did it to Me"?

VIII

AT THE MEETING OF THE SANHEDRIN

Judas Sells Jesus

It was in the residence of the high priest that the enemies of Jesus held the assembly in which they decided to do away with Him. Caiphas, the high priest, presided over their deliberations.

Although this meeting of the Sanhedrin was not an official one, the members of the council resolved to seize Jesus and put Him to death. Still, fear of the people held them back from carrying out their plans immediately: they decided to wait until after the festival ceremonies were ended. An unforeseen incident altered these plans and hastened events. This was the betrayal of Our Lord by Judas Iscariot.

St. Matthew relates the events of this day in the following words: "Then were gathered together the chief priests and ancients of the people into the court of the high priest, who was called Caiphas:

"And they consulted together, that by subtilty they might apprehend Jesus, and put Him to death.

THE MEETING OF THE SANHEDRIN

THE JOURNEYS OF JESUS

"But they said: Not on the festival day, lest perhaps there should be a tumult among the people." (St. Matthew xxvi, 3–5.)

"Then went one of the Twelve, who was called Judas Iscariot, to the chief priests,

"And said to them: What will you give me, and I will deliver Him unto you? But they appointed him thirty pieces of silver.

"And from thenceforth he sought opportunity to betray Him." (St. Matthew xxvi, 14–16.)

QUESTIONS

1. Who was Caiphas?

2. Why did the members of the council hesitate to seize Jesus on the festival day?

3. Quote the words of Judas in trying to sell Jesus.

4. Did the Apostle succeed in selling his Master?

IX

IN JERUSALEM

Peter and John Secure the Dining Room

"And the day of the unleavened bread came, on which it was necessary that the Pasch should be killed.

"And He sent Peter and John, saying: Go, and prepare for us the Pasch, that we may eat.

"But they said: Where wilt Thou that we prepare?

"And He said to them: Behold, as you go into the city, there shall meet you a man carrying a pitcher of water: follow him into the house where he entereth in.

"And you shall say to the goodman of the house: The Master saith to thee, Where is the guest chamber, where I may eat the Pasch with My disciples?

"And he will show you a large dining room, furnished; and there prepare.

"And they going, found as He had said to them, and made ready the Pasch." (St. Luke xxii, 7–13.)

Then the two Apostles hastened back to Bethania to Jesus and the other Apostles.

QUESTIONS

1. What is the meaning of "unleavened bread"?

2. Do you think the "goodman of the house" was a personal friend of Jesus?

THE PASCHAL LAMB

The Apostles secured a yearling lamb, and had it slaughtered at the Temple, as was the custom. The lamb, roasted and seasoned with bitter herbs, was eaten at this great feast, in commemoration of the delivery of the Jews from the hand of Pharaoh, when they were led out of Egypt by their great leader, Moses.

The lamb was the chief part of the meal of remembrance, but there were also wild lettuce and wine, and unleavened bread. The bread was such an important part of the supper that the Passover was also known as the Feast of Azymes, or of the Unleavened Bread.

At this Last Supper, Our Lord Himself was the true Paschal Lamb, though at that time no one knew this but He.

X

IN THE DINING ROOM IN JERUSALEM

The Paschal Feast

When evening came Jesus left Bethania with His disciples and came to the city to the place which He had indicated. Followed by His twelve Apostles, He entered and found everything prepared.

After sunset, at the hour appointed for the Feast, "He sat down, and the twelve Apostles with Him." He occupied the place of honor. The hour was come, and the heart of Jesus was filled with gladness. Seeing Himself surrounded by His followers, Jesus uttered these words in which joy and grief are mingled: "With desire I have desired to eat this Pasch with you, before I suffer."

Yet to make the Apostles understand that it was not this Jewish ceremony for which He had longed so intensely, but rather the accomplishment of a real sacrifice of Himself, He added: "For I say to you, that from this time I will not eat it, till it be fulfilled in the Kingdom of God." (St. Luke xxii, 15–16.)

Jesus was moved and saddened by the thought that

this Passover was to be the last. Yet, in the closing hours of His life He was to give still further proof of His love for His disciples. He had kept until the last the greatest gift of all—the Blessed Eucharist, the Sacrament of His love. This He was to institute and to leave to the world before the end.

QUESTION

Do you think it was the Paschal supper that Christ meant, when He said: "With desire I have desired to eat this Pasch with you, before I suffer"?

Jesus Washes the Feet of His Apostles

All four Evangelists give us the story of the Last Supper, but only St. John relates the touching incident of the washing of the feet of the Apostles by our Blessed Lord. St. John tells us how Our Lord rose from the table, laid aside His garments, girded Himself with a towel, poured water into a basin, and made ready to wash the feet of His disciples.

"He cometh therefore to Simon Peter. And Peter saith to Him: Lord, dost Thou wash my feet?

"Jesus answered, and said to him: What I do thou knowest not now; but thou shalt know hereafter.

"Peter saith to Him: Thou shalt never wash my feet. Jesus answered him: If I wash thee not, thou shalt have no part with Me."

[60]

THE LAST SUPPER

At once Peter understood what these words meant, and with his usual unbounded fervor, he said: "Lord, not only my feet, but also my hands and my head.

"Jesus saith to him: He that is washed, needeth not but to wash his feet, but is clean wholly. And you are clean, but not all." (St. John xiii, 4–10.)

QUESTIONS

1. Which of the Apostles objected to having his feet washed by the Master?

2. Does this cleansing suggest to you any special preparation that should be made before Communion?

A WARNING TO JUDAS

"And you are clean, but not all." In these words Our Lord was referring to Judas, for He knew who he was that would betray Him. But Judas took no notice of the words; he permitted his Lord to kneel before him, pour the water upon his feet, and press them between His hands, and still he remained unmoved.

After His great lesson of love and humility—the washing of feet—was finished, Jesus took His garments and went to His place at the table. When He sat down again, He said to them: "Know you what I have done to you?

"LORD, NOT ONLY MY FEET, BUT ALSO MY HANDS AND MY HEAD"

"You call Me Master, and Lord; and you say well, for so I am.

"If then I being your Lord and Master, have washed your feet; you also ought to wash one another's feet.

"For I have given you an example, that as I have done to you, so you do also.

"Amen, amen I say to you: The servant is not greater than His Lord; neither is the Apostle greater than He that sent him.

"If you know these things, you shall be blessed if you do them.

"I speak not of you all: I know whom I have chosen. But that the Scripture may be fulfilled: *He that eateth bread with Me, shall lift up his heel against Me.*

"At present I tell you, before it come to pass: that when it shall come to pass, you may believe that I am He.

"Amen, amen I say to you, he that receiveth whomsoever I send, receiveth Me; and he that receiveth Me, receiveth Him that sent Me." (St. John xiii, 11–20.)

By these last words Jesus sought to impress upon the Apostles the high dignity to which they had been raised—a dignity so great that those who received them, received Him, and thereby the Father Who sent Him.

IN THE DINING ROOM IN JERUSALEM

QUESTIONS

1. Jesus said: "If you know these things, you shall be blessed if you do them." What did He mean by "these things"?

2. Are there recorded in this chapter any words of Jesus which give encouragement to those who labor for the sick and the poor?

3. Quote the encouraging words.

The Sign of the Betrayer

St. Matthew tells us that while Our Lord and His followers were seated at table Jesus said: "Amen I say to you, that one of you is about to betray Me."

Imagine the astonishment which such an announcement caused among the Apostles! Even the guilty one—perhaps he more than any of the rest—was astounded at this revelation of unfaithfulness and of betrayal.

"And they being very much troubled, began every one to say: Is it I, Lord?

"But He answering, said: He that dippeth his hand with Me in the dish, he shall betray Me.

"The Son of Man indeed goeth, as it is written of Him: but woe to that man by whom the Son of Man shall be betrayed: it were better for him, if that man had not been born.

[65]

"And Judas that betrayed Him, answering, said: Is it I, Rabbi? He saith to him: Thou hast said it." (St. Matthew xxvi, 21–25.)

In spite of this warning, given directly to Judas though probably not heard by the others, the traitor remained at the table to partake of the Pasch.

QUESTIONS

1. Was Judas given a chance to repent after he had sold Jesus?

2. In what words did Jesus let Judas know that He knew his evil purpose of betraying Him?

THE INSTITUTION OF THE BLESSED EUCHARIST

"And whilst they were at supper, Jesus took bread, and blessed, and broke: and gave to His disciples, and said: Take ye, and eat. This is My Body.

"And taking the chalice, He gave thanks, and gave to them, saying: Drink ye all of this.

"For this is My Blood of the new testament, which shall be shed for many unto remission of sins." (St. Matthew xxvi, 26–28.)

"And whilst they were eating, Jesus took bread; and blessing, broke, and gave to them, and said: Take ye. This is My Body.

"And having taken the chalice, giving thanks, He gave it to them. And they all drank of it.

IN THE DINING ROOM IN JERUSALEM

"And He said to them: This is My Blood of the new testament, which shall be shed for many." (St. Mark xiv, 22-24.)

"And taking bread, He gave thanks, and brake; and gave to them, saying: This is My Body, which is given for you. Do this for a commemoration of Me.

"In like manner the chalice also, after He had supped, saying: This is the chalice, the new testament in My Blood, which shall be shed for you." (St. Luke xxii, 19-20.)

Thus in different versions, but all alike in meaning, three of the Evangelists, Matthew, Mark, and Luke, record the institution of the Blessed Eucharist.

The Scripture has still another passage in which St. Paul (1 Corinthians xi, 23-25) says: ". . . the Lord Jesus, the same night in which He was betrayed, took bread,

"And giving thanks, broke, and said: Take ye, and eat: this is My Body, which shall be delivered for you: this do for the commemoration of Me.

"In like manner also the chalice, after He had supped, saying: This chalice is the new testament in My Blood: this do ye, as often as you shall drink, for the commemoration of Me."

The Jews, who had heard Jesus speak of Himself as the Bread of Life, had found it hard to believe that Our Lord would give the world His flesh to

[67]

eat; but at the Last Supper this saying was made true. This promise was fulfilled; and from henceforth His faithful followers would find in His Body and Blood, the food for their souls.

QUESTIONS

1. On what two occasions did Jesus promise to give the world His Body and Blood to be eaten and drunk?

2. On what occasion did He give It to the Apostles?

3. What two Sacraments of the Catholic Church were instituted at the Last Supper?

4. Quote the words of their institution.

THE DEPARTURE OF JUDAS

"When Jesus had said these things, He was troubled in spirit; and He testified, and said: Amen, amen I say to you, one of you shall betray Me."

This second allusion to treason in their own ranks startled the Apostles and they "therefore looked one upon another, doubting of whom He spoke.

"Now there was leaning on Jesus' bosom one of His disciples, whom Jesus loved.

"Simon Peter therefore beckoned to him, and said to him: Who is it of whom He speaketh?

"He therefore, leaning on the breast of Jesus, saith to Him: Lord, who is it?

IN THE DINING ROOM IN JERUSALEM

"Jesus answered: He it is to whom I shall reach bread dipped. And when He had dipped the bread, He gave it to Judas Iscariot, the son of Simon.

"And after the morsel, Satan entered into him. And Jesus said to him: That which thou dost, do quickly.

"Now no man at the table knew to what purpose He said this unto him.

"For some thought, because Judas had the purse, that Jesus had said to him: Buy those things which we have need of for the festival day: or that he should give something to the poor.

"He therefore having received the morsel, went out immediately. And it was night." (St. John xiii, 21–30.)

QUESTIONS

1. In what words did St. John describe the departure of Judas from the dining room?

2. "And it was night." Could St. John have meant that it was night in the soul of Judas as well as nighttime?

A New Commandment

Several chapters of the Gospel of St. John are given up to the words of our Blessed Lord to His Apostles after the institution of the Holy Eucharist and the departure of Judas from the dining room which his presence so dishonored. Every word of Our Lord is precious to those who believe in Him, but in this book we must content ourselves with giving only a few of the striking things He said to His Apostles on this occasion.

When Judas had gone out, Our Saviour said: "Now is the Son of Man glorified, and God is glorified in Him.

"If God be glorified in Him, God also will glorify Him in Himself; and immediately will He glorify Him.

"Little children, yet a little while I am with you. You shall seek Me; and as I said to the Jews: Whither I go you cannot come; so I say to you now."

Jesus then entrusted them with His last wishes: "A new commandment I give unto you: That you love one another, as I have loved you, that you also love one another.

"By this shall all men know that you are My disciples, if you have love one for another." (St. John xiii, 31–35.)

QUESTIONS

1. By what sign were the disciples of Jesus to be known?

2. By what loving name did Jesus call His Apostles?

3. Upon this occasion, what new commandment did Jesus give to His Apostles?

IN THE DINING ROOM IN JERUSALEM

Peter's Boast

"Simon Peter saith to Him: Lord, whither goest Thou? Jesus answered: Whither I go, thou canst not follow Me now; but thou shalt follow hereafter.

"Peter saith to Him: Why cannot I follow Thee now? I will lay down my life for Thee.

"Jesus answered him: Wilt thou lay down thy life for Me? Amen, amen I say to thee, the cock shall not crow, till thou deny Me thrice." (St. John xiii, 36–38.)

Jesus Prays for Peter

The part which St. Peter played in Our Lord's last hours on earth was not an heroic one. Our Saviour had chosen him as the leader of the Apostles, yet when the test came, he broke down and denied his Saviour. Nevertheless the words of Christ to Peter at this time show clearly that this man who would prove to be a coward when his Master was seized, would in the end conquer his fears and prove his leadership.

In view of the fact that St. Peter was to be the head of the Church on earth, very striking and significant were Our Lord's words to him, on this the last day of His earthly life:

"Simon, Simon, behold Satan hath desired to have you, that he may sift you as wheat:

[71]

THE JOURNEYS OF JESUS

"But I have prayed for thee, that thy faith fail not:
and thou, being once converted, confirm thy brethren.

"Who said to Him: Lord, I am ready to go with
Thee, both into prison, and to death.

"And He said: I say to thee, Peter, the cock shall
not crow this day, till thou thrice deniest that thou
knowest Me. And He said to them:

"When I sent you without purse, and scrip, and
shoes, did you want any thing?

"But they said: Nothing. Then said He unto
them: But now he that hath a purse, let him take
it, and likewise a scrip; and he that hath not, let him
sell his coat, and buy a sword.

"For I say to you, that this that is written must
yet be fulfilled in Me: *And with the wicked was he
reckoned.* For the things concerning Me have an end.

"But they said: Lord, behold here are two swords.
And He said to them, It is enough." (St. Luke xxii,
31–38.)

The Apostles did not understand His words so He
tried to strengthen them for the coming conflict.

QUESTIONS

1. St. Peter denied Our Lord. Did his faith in Him
ever fail?

2. Do repentance and hope of forgiveness show faith
in God?

IN THE DINING ROOM IN JERUSALEM

The Way, the Truth, and the Life

Jesus then went on to say to the whole group of the Apostles: "Let not your heart be troubled. You believe in God, believe also in Me.

"In My Father's house there are many mansions. If not, I would have told you: because I go to prepare a place for you.

"And if I shall go, and prepare a place for you, I will come again, and will take you to Myself; that where I am, you also may be.

"And whither I go you know, and the way you know.

"Thomas saith to Him: Lord, we know not whither Thou goest; and how can we know the way?

"Jesus saith to him: I am the Way, and the Truth, and the Life. No man cometh to the Father, but by Me.

"If you had known Me, you would without doubt have known My Father also: and from henceforth you shall know Him, and you have seen Him.

"Philip saith to Him: Lord, show us the Father, and it is enough for us.

"Jesus saith to him: Have I been so long a time with you; and have you not known Me? Philip, he that seeth Me seeth the Father also. How sayest thou, Show us the Father?

[73]

THE JOURNEYS OF JESUS

"Do you not believe, that I am in the Father, and the Father in Me? The words that I speak to you, I speak not of Myself. But the Father Who abideth in Me, He doth the works.

"Believe you not that I am in the Father, and the Father in Me?

"Otherwise believe for the very works' sake." (St. John xiv, 1–12.)

QUESTIONS

1. Quote the words of St. Thomas to Jesus.

2. Do the words of St. Thomas show that he correctly understood Our Lord's words on this occasion?

3. Explain what Christ meant by saying: "I am the Way, and the Truth, and the Life."

THE POWER OF HIS NAME

"Amen, amen I say to you, he that believeth in Me, the works that I do, he also shall do; and greater than these shall he do.

"Because I go to the Father: and whatsoever you shall ask the Father in My Name, that will I do: that the Father may be glorified in the Son.

"If you shall ask Me any thing in My Name, that I will do.

"If you love Me, keep My commandments.

"And I will ask the Father, and He shall give

[74]

you another Paraclete, that He may abide with you for ever.

"The Spirit of Truth, whom the world cannot receive, because it seeth Him not, nor knoweth Him: but you shall know Him; because He shall abide with you, and shall be in you.

"I will not leave you orphans, I will come to you.

"Yet a little while: and the world seeth Me no more. But you see Me: because I live, and you shall live.

"In that day you shall know, that I am in My Father, and you in Me, and I in you.

"He that hath My commandments, and keepeth them; he it is that loveth Me. And he that loveth Me, shall be loved of My Father: and I will love him, and will manifest Myself to him.

"Judas saith to Him, not the Iscariot: Lord, how is it, that Thou wilt manifest Thyself to us, and not to the world?

"Jesus answered, and said to him: If any one love Me, he will keep My Word, and My Father will love him, and We will come to him, and will make Our abode with him.

"He that loveth Me not, keepeth not My words. And the Word which you have heard, is not Mine; but the Father's Who sent Me.

[75]

"These things have I spoken to you, abiding with you.

"But the Paraclete, the Holy Ghost, Whom the Father will send in My Name, He will teach you all things, and bring all things to your mind, whatsoever I shall have said to you." (St. John xiv, 12–26.)

QUESTIONS

1. Quote the verse in which the three Persons of the Blessed Trinity are named.

2. How can one know that he loves God?

A Solemn Farewell

It is an Eastern custom to wish "peace" on meeting and leaving friends. The Apostles were Our Lord's friends and He wanted them to know that His farewell words were not empty sounds, but a real, effective wish.

He said to them therefore: "Peace I leave with you, My peace I give unto you: not as the world giveth, do I give unto you. Let not your heart be troubled, nor let it be afraid.

"You have heard that I said to you: I go away, and I come unto you. If you loved Me, you would indeed be glad, because I go to the Father: for the Father is greater than I.

[76]

IN THE DINING ROOM IN JERUSALEM

"And now I have told you before it come to pass: that when it shall come to pass, you may believe.

"I will not now speak many things with you. For the prince of this world cometh, and in Me he hath not any thing.

"But that the world may know, that I love the Father: and as the Father hath given Me commandment, so do I: Arise, let us go hence." (St. John xiv, 27–31.)

QUESTIONS

1. Jesus said: "If you loved Me, you would indeed be glad, because I go to the Father." Why should they have been glad?

2. Why did Jesus tell the Apostles beforehand that He would leave them, even though the knowledge caused them sorrow?

XI

ON THE WAY TO GETHSEMANI

The True Vine

After this last supper with His Apostles, Our Lord took His way toward the garden of Gethsemani; and His Apostles followed Him closely. As if He were reminded by the vine-clad country through which they passed, Our Lord spoke to His Apostles this parable: "I am the true Vine; and My Father is the Husbandman.

"Every branch in Me, that beareth not fruit, He will take away: and every one that beareth fruit, He will purge it, that it may bring forth more fruit.

"Now you are clean by reason of the Word, which I have spoken to you.

"Abide in Me, and I in you. As the branch cannot bear fruit of itself, unless it abide in the vine, so neither can you, unless you abide in Me.

"I am the Vine; you the branches: he that abideth in Me, and I in him, the same beareth much fruit: for without Me you can do nothing.

"If any one abide not in Me, he shall be cast forth as a branch, and shall wither, and they shall gather him up, and cast him into the fire, and he burneth.

"If you abide in Me, and My words abide in you, you shall ask whatever you will, and it shall be done unto you.

"In this is My Father glorified; that you bring forth very much fruit, and become My disciples.

"As the Father hath loved Me, I also have loved you. Abide in My love.

"If you keep My commandments, you shall abide in My love; and I also have kept My Father's commandments, and do abide in His love.

"These things I have spoken to you, that My joy may be in you, and your joy may be filled." (St. John xv, 1–11.)

Jesus assured His Apostles that if they remained united in spirit and mind they would thus glorify His heavenly Father, enjoy an intimate union with Him, their Saviour, and obtain answer to their united prayers.

QUESTIONS

1. Show in what way the words "you [are] the branches" can be applied to us.

2. Can a branch which is separated from the vine bring forth fruit?

3. In what way can a Christian bring forth fruits worthy of eternal life?

THE JOURNEYS OF JESUS

I Have Called you Friends

"This is My commandment, that you love one another, as I have loved you.

"Greater love than this no man hath, that a man lay down his life for his friends.

"You are My friends, if you do the things that I command you.

"I will not now call you servants: for the servant knoweth not what his lord doth. But I have called you friends: because all things whatsoever I have heard of My Father, I have made known to you.

"You have not chosen Me: but I have chosen you; and have appointed you, that you should go, and should bring forth fruit; and your fruit should remain: that whatsoever you shall ask of the Father in My Name, He may give it you.

"These things I command you, that you love one another." (St. John xv, 12–17.)

QUESTIONS

1. If we do not keep God's commandments, can we truthfully say that we love Him?

2. Can you name the Ten Commandments of God?

3. What is the greatest love that a man can have for his fellow men?

4. Did Christ die only for those who were His friends?

ON THE WAY TO GETHSEMANI

A Little While

"A little while, and now you shall not see Me; and again a little while, and you shall see Me: because I go to the Father.

"Then some of His disciples said one to another: What is this that He saith to us: A little while, and you shall not see Me; . . . because I go to the Father?

"They said therefore: What is this that He saith, A little while? we know not what He speaketh.

"And Jesus knew that they had a mind to ask Him; and He said to them: Of this do you inquire among yourselves, because I said: A little while, and you shall not see Me; and again a little while, and you shall see Me?

"Amen, amen I say to you, that you shall lament and weep, but the world shall rejoice; and you shall be made sorrowful, but your sorrow shall be turned into joy.

"A woman, when she is in labor, hath sorrow, because her hour is come; but when she hath brought forth the child, she remembereth no more the anguish, for joy that a man is born into the world.

"So also you now indeed have sorrow; but I will see you again, and your heart shall rejoice; and your joy no man shall take from you." (St. John xvi, 16–22.)

[81]

THE JOURNEYS OF JESUS

QUESTIONS

1. What do you think was meant by the words "a little while, and now you shall not see Me; and again a little while, and you shall see Me"?

2. Why did Christ leave many things unsaid to the Apostles?

3. How was the Apostles' sorrow later "turned into joy"?

4. When were the Apostles to see Jesus again?

THE MISSION OF THE HOLY GHOST

The words of Our Lord to His Apostles are full of tenderness and consolation, and although He prophesied that they would be called upon to suffer for His sake, He bade them be confident in their prayer. He said: "Amen, amen I say to you: if you ask the Father any thing in My Name, He will give it you.

"Hitherto you have not asked any thing in My Name. Ask, and you shall receive; that your joy may be full.

"These things I have spoken to you in proverbs. The hour cometh, when I will no more speak to you in proverbs, but will show you plainly of the Father.

"In that day you shall ask in My Name; and I say not to you, that I will ask the Father for you;

ON THE WAY TO GETHSEMANI

"For the Father Himself loveth you, because you have loved Me, and have believed that I came out from God.

"I came forth from the Father, and am come into the world: again I leave the world, and I go to the Father.

"His disciples say to Him: Behold, now Thou speakest plainly, and speakest no proverb.

"Now we know that Thou knowest all things, and Thou needest not that any man should ask Thee. By this we believe that Thou camest forth from God.

"Jesus answered them: Do you now believe?

"Behold, the hour cometh, and it is now come, that you shall be scattered every man to his own, and shall leave Me alone; and yet I am not alone, because the Father is with Me.

"These things I have spoken to you, that in Me you may have peace. In the world you shall have distress: but have confidence, I have overcome the world." (St. John xvi, 23–33.)

QUESTIONS

1. To what acts of the Apostles do these words refer: "You . . . shall leave Me alone"?

2. In Whose Name should we ask for all things needful for soul and body?

The Second Prediction of Peter's Denial

"Then Jesus saith to them: All you shall be scandalized in Me this night. For it is written: *I will strike the shepherd, and the sheep of the flock shall be dispersed.*

"But after I shall be risen again, I will go before you into Galilee.

"And Peter answering, said to Him: Although all shall be scandalized in Thee, I will never be scandalized.

"Jesus said to him: Amen I say to thee, that in this night before the cock crow, thou wilt deny Me thrice.

"Peter saith to Him: Yea, though I should die with Thee, I will not deny Thee. And in like manner said all the disciples." (St. Matthew xxvi, 31–35.)

QUESTIONS

1. What boast had Peter made at the Last Supper?

2. Quote the words of Jesus upon the occasion of the first prediction of Peter's denial.

XII

IN GETHSEMANI

The Garden

The garden of Gethsemani lies directly east of the city of Jerusalem and northeast of the Cenacle, or dining room where the Last Supper was held. The Brook of Cedron, dry in summer, becomes a raging torrent in the rainy season; it flows down through the valley of Jehosophat, between Jerusalem and Mount Olivet.

The ancient olive trees of Gethsemani are either the actual trees of the time of Christ or have sprung from them. They are held in great veneration by the faithful. The Franciscan Fathers have built a wall round them to prevent pilgrims anxious for relics from destroying them.

The Prayers and Agony of Jesus

"*Then Jesus came with them into a country place* which is called Gethsemani; and He said to His disciples: Sit you here, till I go yonder and pray.

"And taking with Him Peter and the two sons of Zebedee, He began to grow sorrowful and to be sad.

THE JOURNEYS OF JESUS

"Then He saith to them: My soul is sorrowful even unto death: stay you here, and watch with Me.

"And going a little further, He fell upon His face, praying, and saying: My Father, if it be possible, let this chalice pass from Me. Nevertheless not as I will, but as Thou wilt.

"And He cometh to His disciples, and findeth them asleep, and He saith to Peter: What? Could you not watch one hour with Me?

"Watch ye, and pray that ye enter not into temptation. The spirit indeed is willing, but the flesh weak.

"Again the second time, He went and prayed, saying: My Father, if this chalice may not pass away, but I must drink it, Thy will be done.

"And He cometh again, and findeth them sleeping: for their eyes were heavy.

"And leaving them, He went again: and He prayed the third time, saying the selfsame word.

"Then He cometh to His disciples, and saith to them: Sleep ye now and take your rest; behold the hour is at hand, and the Son of Man shall be betrayed into the hands of sinners.

"Rise, let us go: behold he is at hand that will betray Me." (St. Matthew xxvi, 36–46.)

Jesus was still speaking when an armed band halted near the garden and awaited the signal—a treacherous kiss which Judas was to give His Master.

PRAYER AND AGONY OF JESUS IN THE GARDEN

THE JOURNEYS OF JESUS

QUESTIONS

1. How did the three chosen Apostles fail Jesus?

2. Contrast the conduct of St. Peter at the Last Supper and his conduct in the garden of Gethsemani.

3. How many times did Jesus awaken the three Apostles?

4. In what way was the flock dispersed when the Shepherd was taken?

The Bloody Sweat

When Our Saviour left the three Apostles the last time before Judas came to take Him it was to become more sad and lonely and to suffer the greatest anguish. From the Gospel account we know that not only were His sacred eyes dimmed with tears, but also with blood which poured from His Sacred Body. St. Luke (xxii, 43–44) tells us that "being in an agony, He prayed the longer. And His sweat became as drops of blood, trickling down upon the ground."

The Traitor's Kiss

"And Judas also, who betrayed Him, knew the place; because Jesus had often resorted thither together with His disciples." (St. John xviii, 2.)

"HAIL, RABBI. AND HE KISSED HIM"

"As He yet spoke, behold Judas, one of the Twelve, came, and with him a great multitude with swords and clubs, sent from the chief priests and the ancients of the people.

"And he that betrayed Him, gave them a sign, saying: Whomsoever I shall kiss, that is He, hold Him fast.

"And forthwith coming to Jesus, he said: Hail, Rabbi. And he kissed Him.

"And Jesus said to him: Friend, whereto art thou come? Then they came up, and laid hands on Jesus, and held Him.

"And behold one of them that were with Jesus, stretching forth his hand, drew out his sword: and striking the servant of the high priest, cut off his ear." (St. Matthew xxvi, 47–51.)

"And the name of the servant was Malchus." (St. John xviii, 10.)

When Jesus "had touched his ear, He healed him." (St. Luke xxii, 51.)

And then Jesus turned to him who had committed the deed and said:

"Put up again thy sword into its place: for all that take the sword shall perish with the sword.

"Thinkest thou that I cannot ask My Father, and He will give Me presently more than twelve legions of angels?

"How then shall the Scriptures be fulfilled, that so it must be done?

"In that same hour Jesus said to the multitudes: You are come out as it were to a robber with swords and clubs to apprehend Me. I sat daily with you, teaching in the Temple, and you laid not hands on Me.

"Now all this was done, that the Scriptures of the prophets might be fulfilled. Then the disciples all leaving Him, fled." (St. Matthew xxvi, 52–56.)

QUESTIONS

1. How did Judas know where to find Jesus when he went to betray Him?

2. Find out which Apostle drew his sword and cut off the ear of a servant of the high priest.

3. What miracle did Jesus perform on this occasion?

4. Which of the Evangelists relates the story of this miracle of healing?

XIII

AT THE PALACE OF THE HIGH PRIEST

JESUS BEFORE ANNAS

From Gethsemani the soldiers, with Jesus in their midst, followed the road leading by one of its southern gates into the city of Jerusalem, and came to the house of Annas.

Although Annas had been deposed by the Romans from his place as high priest, yet he managed to preserve an authority in public affairs. He had succeeded in keeping the sovereign priesthood in his family, Caiphas the high priest at that time being his son-in-law. His influence at the time was very powerful. It was before Annas, therefore, that Jesus was first brought; although Annas and Caiphas were each living in a palace at either end of a court, probably within the same inclosure.

It was shortly after midnight when the soldiers with their Prisoner reached the house of Annas, who, in the minds of his countrymen, always remained the only legitimate high priest of the Jewish people, and Jesus, deserted by His disciples, stood before Annas.

AT THE PALACE OF THE HIGH PRIEST

ANNAS QUESTIONS JESUS

Annas was a man learned in the Jewish law; he was old and experienced; therefore he thought he would be doing a great service to the Council if he could get Jesus to give him answers which would prove Him deserving of death. Annas therefore asked Jesus "of His disciples, and of His Doctrine." He wished to prove to Pilate that Jesus had secretly been gathering a powerful and dangerous party and he hoped to be able to convict Him of breaking the Law of Moses.

"Jesus answered him: I have spoken openly to the world: I have always taught in the synagogue, and in the Temple, whither all the Jews resort; and in secret I have spoken nothing.

"Why askest thou Me? ask them who have heard what I have spoken unto them: behold they know what things I have said.

"And when He had said these things, one of the servants standing by, gave Jesus a blow, saying: Answerest Thou the high priest so?

"Jesus answered him: If I have spoken evil, give testimony of the evil; but if well, why strikest thou Me?

"And Annas sent Him bound to Caiphas the high priest." (St. John xviii, 19–24.)

THE JOURNEYS OF JESUS

QUESTIONS

1. Had Annas any right or authority to question or examine Jesus?

2. What outrage did Jesus suffer in the house of Annas?

3. Quote the words of Jesus to the servant.

PETER'S DENIALS

Although Peter had fled with the rest of the disciples when his Master was arrested, the great love which he bore Our Saviour to some extent overcame his fear, so that he followed "afar off" the soldiers and the others who were taking Jesus to the house of Annas.

"And when they had kindled a fire in the midst of the hall, and were sitting about it, Peter was in the midst of them.

"Whom when a certain servant maid had seen sitting at the light, and had earnestly beheld him, she said: This man also was with Him.

"But he denied Him, saying: Woman, I know Him not.

"And after a little while, another seeing him, said: Thou also art one of them. But Peter said: O man, I am not.

"And after the space, as it were of one hour,

"WOMAN, I KNOW HIM NOT"

another certain man affirmed, saying: Of a truth, this man was also with Him; for he is also a Galilean.

"And Peter said: Man, I know not what thou sayest. And immediately, as he was yet speaking, the cock crew.

"And the Lord turning looked on Peter. And Peter remembered the word of the Lord, as He had said: Before the cock crow, thou shalt deny Me thrice.

"And Peter going out, wept bitterly." (St. Luke xxii, 54–62.)

QUESTIONS

1. How many times did Peter deny his Lord?

2. Since Peter had been forewarned, how did it happen that he denied his Master?

3. Can you give a reason why Christ permitted Peter to fail Him?

4. Quote the words of Peter at the time of each denial.

5. Do any words in the text give a reason for Peter's "going out" and weeping bitterly?

JESUS BEFORE CAIPHAS

"But they holding Jesus led Him to Caiphas the high priest, where the Scribes and the ancients were assembled. . . .

"AND PETER GOING OUT, WEPT BITTERLY"

"And the chief priests and the whole Council sought false witness against Jesus, that they might put Him to death:

"And they found not, whereas many false witnesses had come in. And last of all there came two false witnesses:

"And they said: This man said, I am able to destroy the Temple of God, and after three days to rebuild it.

"And the high priest rising up, said to Him: Answerest Thou nothing to the things which these witness against Thee?

"But Jesus held His peace. And the high priest said to Him: I adjure Thee by the living God, that Thou tell us if Thou be the Christ the Son of God.

"Jesus saith to him: Thou hast said it. Nevertheless I say to you, hereafter you shall see the Son of Man sitting on the right hand of the power of God, and coming in the clouds of heaven.

"Then the high priest rent his garments, saying: He hath blasphemed; what further need have we of witnesses? Behold, now you have heard the blasphemy:

"What think you? But they answering, said: He is guilty of death.

"Then did they spit in His face, and buffeted Him:

and others struck His face with the palms of their hands,

"Saying: Prophesy unto us, O Christ, who is he that struck Thee?" (St. Matthew xxvi, 57, 59–68.)

QUESTIONS

1. Jesus at first was silent, but then finally answered Caiphas. Why did He consent to answer the high priest?

2. What is blasphemy?

3. What words of Jesus did the high priest say were blasphemy?

4. What caused them to say, "He is guilty of death"?

5. Jesus had said: "Destroy this Temple, and in three days I will raise it up," meaning the Temple of His Body. Can you recall when He spoke these words?

6. Read St. John iii.

XIV

ON THE MORNING AFTER THE BETRAYAL

THE DESPAIR AND DEATH OF JUDAS

"And when morning was come, all the chief priests and ancients of the people took counsel against Jesus, that they might put Him to death.

"And they brought Him bound, and delivered Him to Pontius Pilate the governor.

"Then Judas, who betrayed Him, seeing that He was condemned, repenting himself, brought back the thirty pieces of silver to the chief priests and ancients,

"Saying: I have sinned in betraying innocent blood. But they said: What is that to us? look thou to it.

"And casting down the pieces of silver in the Temple, he departed: and went and hanged himself with an halter.

"But the chief priests having taken the pieces of silver, said: It is not lawful to put them into the corbona, because it is the price of blood.

"And after they had consulted together, they

bought with them the potter's field, to be a burying place for strangers.

"For this cause that field was called Haceldama, that is, The Field of Blood, even to this day.

"Then was fulfilled that which was spoken by Jeremias the prophet, saying: *And they took the thirty pieces of silver, the price of Him that was prized, Whom they prized of the children of Israel.*

"*And they gave them unto the potter's field, as the Lord appointed to me.*" (St. Matthew xxvii, 1–10.)

The corbona was the treasury in which there were thirteen chests shaped like trumpets. Each chest had an open space to receive the free-will offerings of the people.

Haceldama lies on the southern side of the valley of Hinnom, where it opens into the Cedron valley. It is called the potter's field on account of the clay found there, which is suitable for making pottery. It is still used as a burial ground.

QUESTIONS

1. Judas was filled with remorse and sorrow. What was the difference between his grief and that of St. Peter?

2. Was Judas condemned because he betrayed his Master, or because he despaired of that Master's mercy?

3. What prophet had foretold the use of the money which Judas brought back to the high priest?

XV

IN THE GOVERNOR'S HALL

Jesus before Pilate

"Then they led Jesus from Caiphas to the governor's hall. And it was morning; and they went not into the hall, that they might not be defiled, but that they might eat the Pasch.

"Pilate therefore went out to them, and said: What accusation bring you against this Man?

"They answered, and said to him: If He were not a malefactor, we would not have delivered Him up to thee." (St. John xviii, 28–30.)

"And they began to accuse Him, saying: We have found this Man perverting our nation, and forbidding to give tribute to Cæsar, and saying that He is Christ the King." (St. Luke xxiii, 2.)

"Pilate therefore said to them: Take Him you, and judge Him according to your Law. The Jews therefore said to him: It is not lawful for us to put any man to death;

"That the word of Jesus might be fulfilled, which He said, signifying what death He should die." (St. John xviii, 31–32.)

"WHAT ACCUSATION BRING YOU AGAINST THIS MAN?"

THE JOURNEYS OF JESUS

The Romans had deprived the Jews of all power over human life.

QUESTIONS

1. What accusations were brought against Jesus in the presence of Pilate?

2. How did Pilate receive these false charges?

3. Why was it not lawful for the Jews to put anyone to death?

PILATE QUESTIONS JESUS

"Pilate therefore went into the hall again, and called Jesus, and said to Him: Art Thou the king of the Jews?

"Jesus answered: Sayest thou this thing of thyself, or have others told it thee of Me?

"Pilate answered: Am I a Jew? Thy own nation, and the chief priests, have delivered Thee up to me: what hast Thou done?

"Jesus answered: My Kingdom is not of this world. If My Kingdom were of this world, My servants would certainly strive that I should not be delivered to the Jews: but now My Kingdom is not from hence.

"Pilate therefore said to Him: Art Thou a king then? Jesus answered: Thou sayest that I am a king. For this was I born, and for this came I into the world; that I should give testimony to the Truth. Every one that is of the Truth, heareth My voice.

"Pilate saith to Him: What is truth? And when he said this, he went out again to the Jews, and saith to them: I find no cause in Him." (St. John xviii, 33-38.)

Pontius Pilate

Pontius Pilate was the Roman governor of Judea. He had ruled nearly nine years at the time when he condemned Jesus to death.

Pilate was the first official to bring the Roman soldiers and their barracks into Jerusalem. As the representative of Roman power and law he was naturally not liked by the Jews. It would appear from a passage in St. Luke's Gospel that he was still severe in his treatment of the Jews who were opposed to the Roman rule.

"Pilate," says the Catholic Encyclopedia, "is the type of a worldly man, knowing the right and anxious to do it so far as it can be done without personal sacrifice of any kind, but yielding easily to pressure from those whose interest it is that he should act otherwise. He would gladly have acquitted Christ, and even made serious efforts in that direction, but gave way at once when his own position was threatened."

THE JOURNEYS OF JESUS

Pilate's Wife

Tradition says that Pilate's wife was Claudia Procula, a pious lady of the Roman nobility.

The night before the trial she had been troubled in sleep, and terrible dreams had disturbed her slumbers. Consequently, when she saw Jesus surrounded by the furious mob, and Pilate hesitating and half-determined to condemn Him, she bade some of her servants to take this message to Pilate: "Have thou nothing to do with that just Man; for I have suffered many things this day in a dream because of Him." Here was a special grace sent by God to Pilate. (St. Matthew xxvii, 19.)

The Governor's Hall

The governor's hall, also called the Prætorium, was very likely part of the Castle of Antonia, a strongly built fortress at the northeast corner of the city, north of the Temple and projecting from it. Herod the Great had built the Castle of Antonia, and had named it for his friend, Mark Antony.

The Ecce Homo Arch and the Flagellation Chapel are here, and from this Prætorium, pilgrims at the present day begin the Way of the Cross.

XVI

AT THE COURT OF HEROD

Jesus before Herod

Pilate would have saved Our Lord from the fury of His enemies, if he could have done it without injuring himself. He told the Jews that he found no reason why Our Saviour should be killed, "But they were more earnest, saying: He stirreth up the people, teaching throughout all Judea, beginning from Galilee to this place."

Pilate, catching at the word "Galilee," asked whether the Man were of Galilee. "And when he understood that He was of Herod's jurisdiction, he sent Him away to Herod, who was also himself at Jerusalem, in those days."

Jesus was therefore led from Pilate's court to the court of Herod.

"And Herod seeing Jesus, was very glad; for he was desirous of a long time to see Him, because he had heard many things of Him; and he hoped to see some sign wrought by Him.

"And he questioned Him in many words. But He answered him nothing.

[107]

THE JOURNEYS OF JESUS

"And the chief priests and the Scribes stood by, earnestly accusing Him.

"And Herod with his army set Him at nought, and mocked Him, putting on Him a white garment, and sent Him back to Pilate.

"And Herod and Pilate were made friends, that same day; for before they were enemies one to another." (St. Luke xxiii, 5–12.)

HEROD ANTIPAS

It was to Herod Antipas, ruler under the Romans of the Province of Galilee, that Our Lord was sent by Pilate. This was the same Herod who had put St. John the Baptist to death at the request of Salome, the daughter of Herodias.

Herod Antipas was the son of Herod the Great who, although not of Jewish descent, had been the King of Judea at Our Lord's birth, and who, seeking to kill the new-born Babe of Bethlehem, had caused the slaughter of the Holy Innocents.

QUESTIONS

1. Who was Herod?

2. Give some reasons why Herod was glad to see Jesus.

3. Did Jesus gratify Herod's curiosity by working a miracle before him?

[108]

XVII

IN THE GOVERNOR'S HALL ONCE MORE

Jesus is Led back to Pilate

Herod, adopting Roman customs to please the Roman governor, had dressed Jesus as a mock king, and had sent Him back to Pilate. Pilate's plan to give the responsibility to someone else had failed. He was driven to try a fresh move.

"And Pilate, calling together the chief priests, and the magistrates, and the people,

"Said to them: You have presented unto me this Man, as one that perverteth the people; and behold I, having examined Him before you, find no cause in this Man, in those things wherein you accuse Him.

"No, nor Herod neither. For I sent you to him, and behold, nothing worthy of death is done to Him.

"I will chastise Him therefore, and release Him.

"Now of necessity he was to release unto them one upon the feast day.

"But the whole multitude together cried out, saying: Away with this Man, and release unto us Barabbas:

"Who, for a certain sedition made in the city, and for a murder, was cast into prison.

"And Pilate again spoke to them, desiring to release Jesus.

"But they cried again, saying: Crucify Him, crucify Him.

"And he said to them the third time: Why, what evil hath this Man done? I find no cause of death in Him. I will chastise Him therefore, and let Him go.

"But they were instant with loud voices, requiring that He might be crucified; and their voices prevailed.

"And Pilate gave sentence that it should be as they required.

"And he released unto them him who for murder and sedition, had been cast into prison, whom they had desired; but Jesus he delivered up to their will." (St. Luke xxiii, 13–25.)

QUESTIONS

1. In what words did Pilate declare Christ innocent?

2. Why, if he found Him innocent, did he order Him to be scourged?

3. Hoping to save Jesus from death, what choice of men did Pilate offer the Jews?

4. How did Pilate insult Jesus in proposing this choice? (See also St. John xviii, 39–40.)

IN THE GOVERNOR'S HALL ONCE MORE

"Behold the Man"

In the story of the condemnation of Christ as given by St. John, we are told that before delivering Our Lord to be crucified, Pilate had Jesus scourged by his soldiers. And when they had scourged Him they platted a crown of thorns and put it on His head; and they put on Him a purple garment in mockery. St. Matthew adds that they put a reed in His right hand, in mocking imitation of a kingly sceptre, and that they spat upon Him in derision.

St. John continues: "And they came to Him, and said: Hail, King of the Jews; and they gave Him blows.

"Pilate therefore went forth again, and saith to them: Behold, I bring Him forth unto you, that you may know that I find no cause in Him.

"(Jesus therefore came forth, bearing the crown of thorns and the purple garment.) And he saith to them: Behold the Man.

"When the chief priests, therefore, and the servants, had seen Him, they cried out, saying: Crucify Him, crucify Him. Pilate saith to them: Take Him you, and crucify Him: for I find no cause in Him.

"The Jews answered him: We have a law; and according to the law He ought to die, because He made Himself the Son of God.

"When Pilate therefore had heard this saying, he feared the more.

"And he entered into the hall again, and he said to Jesus: Whence art Thou? But Jesus gave him no answer.

"Pilate therefore saith to Him: Speakest Thou not to me? knowest Thou not that I have power to crucify Thee, and I have power to release Thee?

"Jesus answered: Thou shouldst not have any power against Me, unless it were given thee from above. Therefore, he that hath delivered Me to thee, hath the greater sin.

"And from henceforth Pilate sought to release Him. But the Jews cried out, saying: If thou release this Man, thou art not Cæsar's friend. For whosoever maketh himself a king, speaketh against Cæsar."

Pilate wanted to be a friend to Jesus: yet with all his soul he feared to be reported as no friend to Tiberius Cæsar. Jesus or Cæsar! Which should it be? To his own shame, he chose Cæsar. And so did the Jews; for, when Pilate said to them, "Behold your King," they cried out, "Away with Him; away with Him; crucify Him. Pilate saith to them: Shall I crucify your King? The chief priests answered: We have no king but Cæsar." (St. John xix, 1–15.)

Pilate's crime was one of cowardly weakness. Fear

"BEHOLD THE MAN!"

of future disgrace overmastered every other feeling and he delivered Jesus into their hands.

In a last effort to ease his conscience of the crime of condemning an innocent man to death, he took water, and "washed his hands before the people, saying: I am innocent of the blood of this just Man; look you to it.

"And the whole people answering, said: His blood be upon us and upon our children.

"Then he released to them Barabbas, and having scourged Jesus, delivered Him unto them to be crucified." (St. Matthew xxvii, 24–26.)

QUESTIONS

1. It was in Pilate's power to release Jesus. What prevented him from doing so?

2. By washing his hands before the people, and saying, "I am innocent of the blood of this just Man," was Pilate really without guilt of a great crime?

XVIII

ON THE WAY TO CALVARY

Jesus Takes up His Cross

"And the soldiers led Him away into the court of the palace, and they called together the whole band:

"And they clothe Him with purple, and platting a crown of thorns, they put it upon Him.

"And they began to salute Him: Hail, King of the Jews.

"And they struck His head with a reed: and they did spit on Him. And bowing their knees, they adored Him.

"And after they had mocked Him, they took off the purple from Him, and put His own garments on Him, and they led Him out to crucify Him.

"And they forced one Simon a Cyrenian who passed by, coming out of the country, the father of Alexander and of Rufus, to take up His Cross." (St. Mark xv, 16–21.)

According to Roman custom and law, a centurion was in command of the soldiers on occasions like this. Before the centurion marched a herald who blew a trumpet to open a passage; another officer walked at his side, carrying the title to be placed at the top of the Cross.

QUESTIONS

1. Why did the soldiers force Simon to help Jesus to carry the Cross?

2. Can you think of a reason why they "put His own garments on Him"?

3. In what way did the soldiers mock Jesus?

JESUS AND THE WOMEN OF JERUSALEM

In St. Luke's description of the Passion of Our Lord there are some details which the other three Evangelists do not give. For example, St. Luke gives us this scene which occurred when Jesus was carrying the Cross to Calvary:

"And there followed Him a great multitude of people, and of women, who bewailed and lamented Him.

"But Jesus turning to them, said: Daughters of Jerusalem, weep not over Me; but weep for yourselves, and for your children." (St. Luke xxiii, 27–28.)

Then Jesus predicted the days of sorrow that would come to Jerusalem, because it had not accepted Him and His teachings, but had sent Him to death like a common criminal.

"DAUGHTERS OF JERUSALEM, WEEP NOT OVER ME"

XIX

AT CALVARY

The Crucifixion

"And they bring Him into the place called Golgotha, which being interpreted is, The place of Calvary.

"And they gave Him to drink wine mingled with myrrh; but He took it not.

"And crucifying Him, they divided His garments, casting lots upon them, what every man should take.

"And it was the third hour, and they crucified Him.

"And the inscription of His cause was written over: THE KING OF THE JEWS.

"And with Him they crucify two thieves; the one on His right hand, and the other on His left.

"And the Scripture was fulfilled, which saith: *And with the wicked He was reputed.*

"And they that passed by blasphemed Him, wagging their heads, and saying: Vah, Thou that destroyest the Temple of God, and in three days buildest it up again;

"Save Thyself, coming down from the Cross.

AT CALVARY

"In like manner also the chief priests mocking, said with the Scribes one to another: He saved others; Himself He cannot save.

"Let Christ the King of Israel come down now from the Cross, that we may see and believe. And they that were crucified with Him reviled Him." (St. Mark xv, 22–32.)

St. Luke in his Gospel (xxiii, 34) gives us Our Lord's words of forgiveness for those who were so cruelly torturing Him and reviling Him: "Father, forgive them, for they know not what they do."

QUESTIONS

1. "Father, forgive them, for they know not what they do." What virtue do these words of Jesus teach us?

2. Why did one of those that was crucified with Him revile Him?

THE INSCRIPTION ON THE CROSS

St. John (xix, 19–22) says: "And Pilate wrote a title also, and he put it upon the Cross. And the writing was: JESUS OF NAZARETH, THE KING OF THE JEWS.

"This title therefore many of the Jews did read: because the place where Jesus was crucified was nigh to the city: and it was written in Hebrew, in Greek, and in Latin.

THE JOURNEYS OF JESUS

"Then the chief priests of the Jews said to Pilate: Write not, The King of the Jews; but that He said, I am the King of the Jews.

"Pilate answered: What I have written, I have written."

Another of the Evangelists tells us that "they put over His head His cause written: THIS IS JESUS THE KING OF THE JEWS." (St. Matthew xxvii, 37.)

St. Mark (xv, 26) writes thus: "And the inscription of His cause was written over: THE KING OF THE JEWS."

QUESTIONS

1. What inscription was placed on the Cross?

2. You often see the letters I.N.R.I. on crucifixes. Find out for what these letters stand.

The Soldiers Cast Lots for His Garments

"The soldiers therefore, when they had crucified Him, took His garments, (and they made four parts, to every soldier a part,) and also His coat. Now the coat was without seam, woven from the top throughout.

"They said then one to another: Let us not cut it, but let us cast lots for it, whose it shall be; that the Scripture might be fulfilled, saying: *They have parted My garments among them, and upon My vesture they have cast lot."* (St. John xix, 23–24.)

The garments that the soldiers divided were the sandals, the girdle, the outer robe, and the headdress; the inner garment was of one piece and woven; it was not divided. High priests wore a similar tunic of one piece.

THE REPENTANT THIEF ON THE CROSS

"And the soldiers also mocked Him, coming to Him, and offering Him vinegar,

"And saying: If Thou be the King of the Jews, save Thyself. . . .

"And one of those robbers who were hanged, blasphemed Him, saying: If Thou be Christ, save Thyself and us.

"But the other answering, rebuked him, saying: Neither dost thou fear God, seeing thou art under the same condemnation?

"And we indeed justly, for we receive the due reward of our deeds; but this Man hath done no evil.

"And he said to Jesus: Lord, remember me when Thou shalt come into Thy Kingdom.

"And Jesus said to him: Amen I say to thee, this day thou shalt be with Me in paradise." (St. Luke xxiii, 36–37, 39–43.)

THE JOURNEYS OF JESUS

QUESTIONS

1. What two lessons should we learn from the death of Judas and the death of the repentant thief on the Cross?

2. What is the meaning of these words of the thief on the Cross: "We receive the due reward of our deeds; but this Man hath done no evil"?

"BEHOLD THY SON. BEHOLD THY MOTHER"

Among those who saw our Blessed Lord hanging on the Cross, waiting for death to come, was His Blessed Mother.

All His life the shadow of this fate had hung over Him, and she "who kept all those things in her heart" was conscious of the price that He should one day pay for the sins of men.

Now that the bitter day had at last arrived, we find her at the foot of the Cross, her heart pierced with grief. Near her stands the "beloved disciple," St. John; and as the blood from Our Lord's many wounds bedews the ground, and the weariness of death comes upon Him, He remembers these two who are so dear to Him, and, speaking to Mary, He says: "Woman, behold thy son.

"After that, He saith to the disciple: Behold thy Mother. And from that hour, the disciple took her to his own."

THE CRUCIFIXION

THE JOURNEYS OF JESUS

This Evangelist also tells us that "there stood by the Cross of Jesus, His Mother, His Mother's sister, Mary of Cleophas, and Mary Magdalen." (St. John xix, 25–27.)

QUESTIONS

1. When Christ gave His Blessed Mother into the care and love of St. John, did the act have any meaning for us?

2. In what sense can we say that we are "Children of Mary"?

3. Our Lord loved His Blessed Mother; yet He permitted her to suffer. What should we think if He sends us suffering?

JESUS ON THE CROSS

"And when the sixth hour was come, there was darkness over the whole earth until the ninth hour.

"And at the ninth hour, Jesus cried out with a loud voice, saying: Eloi, Eloi, lamma sabacthani? Which is, being interpreted, My God, My God, why hast Thou forsaken Me?

"And some of the standers by hearing, said: Behold he calleth Elias.

"And one running and filling a sponge with vinegar, and putting it upon a reed, gave Him to drink, saying: Stay, let us see if Elias come to take Him down.

"INDEED THIS MAN WAS THE SON OF GOD"

"And Jesus having cried out with a loud voice, gave up the ghost.

"And the veil of the Temple was rent in two, from the top to the bottom.

"And the centurion who stood over against Him, seeing that crying out in this manner He had given up the ghost, said: Indeed this Man was the Son of God.

"And there were also women looking on afar off: among whom was Mary Magdalen, and Mary the mother of James the Less and of Joseph, and Salome:

"Who also when He was in Galilee followed Him, and ministered to Him, and many other women that came up with Him to Jerusalem." (St. Mark xv, 33–41.)

QUESTIONS

1. Name some extraordinary things that happened when Christ died.

2. Did these extraordinary events bring about any conversions?

3. Who were the first unbelievers to give testimony that Christ is the Son of God?

4. Quote the words of the centurion at the Death of Christ.

5. Do these words give any sign of his faith in Christ?

AT CALVARY

The Death of Jesus

It was at the ninth hour, that is, three o'clock in the afternoon, that Our Saviour died, after hanging three hours upon the Cross.

"And bowing His head, He gave up the ghost." (St. John xix, 30.)

"And Jesus again crying with a loud voice, yielded up the ghost." (St. Matthew xxvii, 50.) St. John also tells us that He said at the end, "It is consummated."

Christ's dying proved that He had a human nature, as His miracles had proved His divinity. In His Death every prophecy concerning the Messias was entirely fulfilled.

At the moment when Christ died, "the veil of the Temple was rent in two from the top even to the bottom, and the earth quaked, and the rocks were rent.

"And the graves were opened: and many bodies of the saints that had slept arose,

"And coming out of the tombs after His Resurrection, came into the Holy City, and appeared to many.

"Now the centurion and they that were with him watching Jesus, having seen the earthquake, and the things that were done, were sore afraid, saying: Indeed this was the Son of God.

THE JOURNEYS OF JESUS

"And there were there many women afar off, who had followed Jesus from Galilee, ministering unto Him:

"Among whom was Mary Magdalen, and Mary the mother of James and Joseph, and the mother of the sons of Zebedee." (St. Matthew xxvii, 51–56.)

And St. Luke (xxiii, 48) says that "all the multitude of them that were come together to that sight, and saw the things that were done, returned striking their breasts."

QUESTIONS

1. In what way did Christ's Death prove that He was human?

2. In what way did He prove that He was divine?

3. Can you name some of those who were standing at the foot of the Cross when Jesus died?

4. Give the words of the seven utterances of Jesus as He hung upon the Cross.

THE HEART OF JESUS IS PIERCED

"Then the Jews, (because it was the parasceve,) that the bodies might not remain upon the Cross on the Sabbath day, (for that was a great Sabbath day,) besought Pilate that their legs might be broken, and that they might be taken away.

"The soldiers therefore came; and they broke the

legs of the first, and of the other that was crucified with Him.

"But after they were come to Jesus, when they saw that He was already dead, they did not break His legs.

"But one of the soldiers with a spear opened His side, and immediately there came out blood and water.

"And he that saw it, hath given testimony; and his testimony is true. And he knoweth that he saith true; that you also may believe.

"For these things were done, that the Scripture might be fulfilled: *You shall not break a bone of Him.*

"And again another Scripture saith: *They shall look on Him Whom they pierced.*" (St. John xix, 31–37.)

QUESTIONS

1. The soldiers broke the legs of the two thieves. Why did they not break those of Jesus?

2. When they saw that Jesus was dead, why did one of the soldiers open His side with a spear?

XX

THE EVENING OF THE CRUCIFIXION

Joseph of Arimathea

As evening approached, a Jew who had not appeared before upon Calvary suddenly presented himself among the soldiers. His name was Joseph of Arimathea, and he was a member of the Sanhedrin which had condemned Jesus.

Rich and powerful, he had lacked courage to declare himself in favor of the Lord because he feared the Sanhedrin, and out of consideration of his own rank. Nevertheless, he was a good and just man and allowed his feelings to be known abroad by firmly refusing any counsel or advice against Jesus. The Master's death had conquered him; and at a time when all were shuddering with fear, a sudden boldness inspired him.

He came to Calvary and there found the soldiers preparing to take down the bodies, in order to bury them, together with the instruments of execution; but he obtained from the centurion who had just confessed his belief in the divinity of Christ a promise

"THEY TOOK THEREFORE THE BODY OF JESUS"

that he would grant the delay which Joseph, the Sanhedrin-Councilor, deemed necessary.

Joseph then returned to Jerusalem in search of Pilate and, when he found him, fearlessly besought him to let him have the Body of Jesus. The Governor's first thought, on learning of the death of Jesus, was one of wonder and astonishment. He could not believe that death would come so quickly to end the torture of Him Whom he had not had the courage to save from the hands of the Jews. Having had the centurion brought to him, he inquired of him whether Jesus was really dead.

Upon hearing a full account of all that had happened on Calvary, he hesitated no longer to put faith in Joseph's word, and willingly granted him the Saviour's Body; for the Romans never refused this consolation to the friends of the condemned.

Joseph therefore proceeded to purchase a linen shroud, a winding sheet, costly oils, and perfumes to be used in the burial of Jesus; then hurried back to Calvary, where, aided by the disciples and his friends, he lifted Jesus down from the Cross.

QUESTION

Did it require courage for Joseph of Arimathea to ask Pilate for the Body of Jesus?

THE EVENING OF THE CRUCIFIXION

The Burial of Jesus by Joseph and Nicodemus

"And after these things, Joseph of Arimathea (because he was a disciple of Jesus, but secretly for fear of the Jews) besought Pilate that he might take away the Body of Jesus. And Pilate gave leave. He came therefore, and took away the Body of Jesus.

"And Nicodemus also came, (he who at the first came to Jesus by night,) bringing a mixture of myrrh and aloes, about an hundred pound weight.

"They took therefore the Body of Jesus, and bound it in linen cloths, with the spices, as the manner of the Jews is to bury." (St. John xix, 38–40.)

The first beams of the stars would announce the beginning of the Sabbath. They must, then, hasten to complete the preparation for the burial.

The Tomb of Our Lord

Our Lord's tomb was hewn out of solid rock. It consists of two parts: an outer vestibule about a yard deep, and an inner room entered through a low, upright doorway. The inner chamber is about nine feet from east to west, and about seven feet from north to south. The height of the room is about nine feet.

The stone bed upon which the Sacred Body was laid stands, as you enter, on the right-hand side of the entrance, from east to west.

3

[133]

THE JOURNEYS OF JESUS

The Guards at the Sepulchre

"Now there was in the place where He was cruci-fied, a garden; and in the garden a new sepulchre, wherein no man yet had been laid.

"There, therefore, because of the parasceve of the Jews, they laid Jesus, because the sepulchre was nigh at hand." (St. John xix, 41–42.)

"And the next day, which followed the day of preparation, the chief priests and the Pharisees came together to Pilate,

"Saying: Sir, we have remembered, that that se-ducer said, while He was yet alive: After three days I will rise again.

"Command therefore the sepulchre to be guarded until the third day: lest perhaps His disciples come and steal Him away, and say to the people: He is risen from the dead; and the last error shall be worse than the first.

"Pilate saith to them: You have a guard; go, guard it as you know.

"And they departing, made the sepulchre sure, sealing the stone, and setting guards." (St. Matthew xxvii, 62–66.)

On the Sabbath day the holy women rested ac-cording to the commandment of Moses. And all that day the Body of Jesus lay in the tomb.

THE EVENING OF THE CRUCIFIXION

Did not the remembrance of the Saviour's prediction—the sign of Jonas the prophet buried three days beneath the waves, then coming forth to a fuller and more complete life—disturb the enemies of Jesus and fill them with anxious fear, lest the mystic Temple not made with hands should appear in three days? Was this not their chief reason for "setting guards" near the entrance to the sepulchre?

QUESTIONS

1. Why were guards placed at the tomb?

2. Find in the Biblical Glossary the meaning of the word *parasceve*.

3. How was the sepulchre made sure?

XXI

THE MORNING OF THE THIRD DAY

The Resurrection

The tomb of Our Lord, carefully closed and sealed, was guarded by Roman soldiers all during the parasceve, the Sabbath day itself, and part of the night preceding the first day of the week. Then something happened which no earthly power could prevent; namely, the glorious Resurrection of our Blessed Lord from the tomb.

The four Evangelists tell the story of this event. Although each tells it differently, the accounts agree in all essentials: the finding of the empty tomb, the Resurrection of Our Saviour, and His appearance to a number of persons.

The Holy Women at the Sepulchre

St. Matthew (xxviii, 1–10) gives us this version of the story: "And in the end of the Sabbath, when it began to dawn towards the first day of the week, came Mary Magdalen and the other Mary, to see the sepulchre.

"FEAR NOT YOU; FOR I KNOW THAT YOU SEEK JESUS WHO WAS CRUCIFIED"

"And behold there was a great earthquake. For an angel of the Lord descended from heaven, and coming, rolled back the stone, and sat upon it.

"And his countenance was as lightning, and his raiment as snow.

"And for fear of him, the guards were struck with terror, and became as dead men.

"And the angel answering, said to the women: Fear not you; for I know that you seek Jesus Who was crucified.

"He is not here, for He is risen, as He said. Come, and see the place where the Lord was laid.

"And going quickly, tell ye His disciples that He is risen: and behold He will go before you into Galilee; there you shall see Him. Lo, I have foretold it to you.

"And they went out quickly from the sepulchre with fear and great joy, running to tell His disciples.

"And behold Jesus met them, saying: All hail. But they came up and took hold of His feet, and adored Him.

"Then Jesus said to them: Fear not. Go, tell My brethren that they go into Galilee, there they shall see Me."

The two women went from the sepulchre in terror. "For a trembling and fear had seized them: and they said nothing to any man; for they were afraid." (St. Mark xvi, 8.)

THE MORNING OF THE THIRD DAY

QUESTIONS

1. Give an account of the visit of the holy women to the sepulchre.

2. Who were these holy women?

3. What were the angel's words to them?

THE GUARDS BRIBED BY THE CHIEF PRIESTS

When the disciples "were departed, behold some of the guards came into the city, and told the chief priests all things that had been done.

"And they being assembled together with the ancients, taking counsel, gave a great sum of money to the soldiers,

"Saying: Say you, His disciples came by night, and stole Him away when we were asleep.

"And if the governor shall hear of this, we will persuade him, and secure you.

"So they taking the money, did as they were taught: and this word was spread abroad among the Jews even unto this day." (St. Matthew xxviii, 11–15.)

QUESTIONS

1. What would be likely to happen to Roman guards who slept while on duty?

2. Is it likely that when the guards were asleep they would know what the disciples were doing?

3. Did these guards fail in their duty?

4. How did their words strengthen the truth of the Resurrection of Christ?

PETER AND JOHN AT THE SEPULCHRE

When Mary Magdalen had seen the empty tomb, she hastened to tell St. Peter and St. John: "They have taken away the Lord out of the sepulchre, and we know not where they have laid Him.

"Peter therefore went out, and that other disciple, and they came to the sepulchre.

"And they both ran together, and that other disciple did outrun Peter, and came first to the sepulchre.

"And when he stooped down, he saw the linen cloths lying; but yet he went not in.

"Then cometh Simon Peter, following him, and went into the sepulchre, and saw the linen cloths lying,

"And the napkin that had been about His head, not lying with the linen cloths, but apart, wrapped up into one place.

"Then that other disciple also went in, who came first to the sepulchre: and he saw, and believed.

"For as yet they knew not the Scripture, that He must rise again from the dead.

"The disciples therefore departed again to their home." (St. John xx, 1–10.)

[140]

THE MORNING OF THE THIRD DAY

QUESTIONS

1. What reason was there for John to remain outside the tomb until Peter came?

2. Of which, Peter or John, is it written that "he saw, and believed."

CHRIST APPEARS TO MARY MAGDALEN

After Mary Magdalen had told the two Apostles about the empty sepulchre, she immediately returned weeping to the grave and peered into the dark cave.

"And she saw two angels in white, sitting, one at the head, and one at the feet, where the Body of Jesus had been laid.

"They say to her: Woman, why weepest thou? She saith to them: Because they have taken away my Lord; and I know not where they have laid Him.

"When she had thus said, she turned herself back, and saw Jesus standing; and she knew not that it was Jesus.

"Jesus saith to her: Woman, why weepest thou? whom seekest thou? She, thinking that it was the gardener, saith to Him: Sir, if thou hast taken Him hence, tell me where thou hast laid Him, and I will take Him away.

"Jesus saith to her: Mary. She turning, saith to Him: Rabboni (which is to say, Master).

"JESUS SAITH TO HER: MARY"

THE MORNING OF THE THIRD DAY

"Jesus saith to her: Do not touch Me, for I am not yet ascended to My Father. But go to My brethren, and say to them: I ascend to My Father and to your Father, to My God and your God.

"Mary Magdalen cometh, and telleth the disciples: I have seen the Lord, and these things He said to me." (St. John xx, 11–18.)

According to this Gospel Mary Magdalen was the first person to whom Our Lord showed Himself on His Resurrection from the tomb, but it has long been a pious belief in the Church that even before He had revealed Himself to her, He had appeared to His Blessed Mother. As His last thought had been for her when He hung dying on the Cross, so it would seem natural to believe that His first thought, in His Risen Body, would be for her also.

QUESTIONS

1. Could Mary Magdalen have taken away the Body of the Lord?

2. Why, then, did she say, "I will take Him away"?

3. Can you give a reason for Christ's appearing to Mary Magdalen before all others except His Blessed Mother?

XXII

TOWARD THE EVENING OF THE THIRD DAY

ON THE ROAD TO EMMAUS

"And behold, two of them went, the same day, to a town which was sixty furlongs from Jerusalem, named Emmaus.

"And they talked together of all these things which had happened.

"And it came to pass, that while they talked and reasoned with themselves, Jesus Himself also drawing near, went with them.

"But their eyes were held, that they should not know Him.

"And He said to them: What are these discourses that you hold one with another as you walk, and are sad?

"And the one of them, whose name was Cleophas, answering, said to Him: Art thou only a stranger in Jerusalem, and hast not known the things that have been done there in these days?

"To whom He said: What things? And they said:

Concerning Jesus of Nazareth, who was a Prophet, mighty in work and word before God and all the people;

"And how our chief priests and princes delivered Him to be condemned to death, and crucified Him.

"But we hoped, that it was He that should have redeemed Israel: and now besides all this, to day is the third day since these things were done.

"Yea and certain women also of our company affrighted us, who before it was light, were at the sepulchre,

"And not finding His Body, came, saying, that they had also seen a vision of angels, who say that He is alive.

"And some of our people went to the sepulchre, and found it so as the women had said, but Him they found not.

"Then He said to them: O foolish, and slow of heart to believe in all things which the prophets have spoken.

"Ought not Christ to have suffered these things, and so to enter into His glory?

"And beginning at Moses and all the prophets, He expounded to them in all the Scriptures, the things that were concerning Him." (St. Luke xxiv, 13–27.)

THE JOURNEYS OF JESUS

JESUS REVEALS HIMSELF TO THE TWO DISCIPLES

"And they drew nigh to the town, whither they were going: and He made as though He would go farther.

"But they constrained Him; saying: Stay with us, because it is towards evening, and the day is now far spent. And He went in with them.

"And it came to pass, whilst He was at table with them, He took bread, and blessed, and brake, and gave to them.

"And their eyes were opened, and they knew Him: and He vanished out of their sight.

"And they said one to the other: Was not our heart burning within us, whilst He spoke in the way, and opened to us the Scriptures?

"And rising up, the same hour, they went back to Jerusalem: and they found the Eleven gathered together, and those that were with them,

"Saying: The Lord is risen indeed, and hath appeared to Simon.

"And they told what things were done in the way; and how they knew Him in the breaking of bread." (St. Luke xxiv, 28–35.)

But their tale did not obtain the same belief as had that of Peter. This Stranger, walking and eating with them, could not be the Risen Lord; so reasoned the troubled Apostles.

"THEY KNEW HIM IN THE BREAKING OF BREAD"

THE JOURNEYS OF JESUS

QUESTIONS

1. Locate Emmaus on the map.

2. Can you relate to the class the story of the two disciples who were on their way to Emmaus?

3. Why does the Gospel say: "And their eyes were opened, and they knew Him"?

4. How did they know Jesus?

5. Why did they go back to Jerusalem?

6. To what place in the city did they go?

7. Whom did they find assembled there?

XXIII

THE EVENING OF THE THIRD DAY

Jesus Appears to the Disciples

"Now whilst they were speaking these things, Jesus stood in the midst of them, and saith to them: Peace be to you; it is I, fear not.

"But they being troubled and frighted, supposed that they saw a spirit.

"And He said to them: Why are you troubled, and why do thoughts arise in your hearts?

"See My hands and feet, that it is I Myself; handle, and see: for a spirit hath not flesh and bones, as you see Me to have.

"And when He had said this, He showed them His hands and feet.

"But while they yet believed not, and wondered for joy, He said: Have you here any thing to eat?

"And they offered Him a piece of a broiled fish, and a honeycomb.

"And when He had eaten before them, taking the remains, He gave to them.

"And He said to them: These are the words which

I spoke to you, while I was yet with you, that all things must needs be fulfilled, which are written in the Law of Moses, and in the Prophets, and in the psalms, concerning Me.

"Then He opened their understanding, that they might understand the Scriptures.

"And He said to them: Thus it is written, and thus it behoved Christ to suffer, and to rise again from the dead, the third day:

"And that penance and remission of sins should be preached in His Name, unto all nations, beginning at Jerusalem." (St. Luke xxiv, 36–47.)

QUESTIONS

1. What was the significance of these words of Jesus: "Have you here any thing to eat"?

2. Why on this evening did Jesus show them His hands and feet, and say: "Handle, and see"?

IN THE DINING ROOM AFTER THE RESURRECTION

"Now when it was late that same day, the first of the week, and the doors were shut, where the disciples were gathered together, for fear of the Jews, Jesus came and stood in the midst, and said to them: Peace be to you.

"And when He had said this, He showed them

"JESUS STOOD IN THE MIDST OF THEM"

His hands and His side. The disciples therefore were glad, when they saw the Lord.

"He said therefore to them again: Peace be to you. As the Father hath sent Me, I also send you.

"When He had said this, He breathed on them; and He said to them: Receive ye the Holy Ghost.

"Whose sins you shall forgive, they are forgiven them; and whose sins you shall retain, they are retained." (St. John xx, 19–23.)

QUESTIONS

1. By what words did Christ institute the Sacrament of Penance?

2. When did Christ say to the assembled Apostles: "Receive ye the Holy Ghost"?

3. Why is it necessary to confess sins in order to have them forgiven?

4. What is the meaning of the words: "Whose sins you shall retain, they are retained"?

XXIV

IN JERUSALEM EIGHT DAYS LATER

Jesus Reveals Himself to Thomas

St. John tells us that St. Thomas was not with the other Apostles when Jesus appeared to them. He joined them later; the joyous disciples greeted him with the words: "We have seen the Lord," and told him about the Master's visit. Doubting the truth of their words, he answered sadly: "Except I shall see in His hands the print of the nails, and put my finger into the place of the nails, and put my hand into His side, I will not believe.

"And after eight days again His disciples were within, and Thomas with them. Jesus cometh, the doors being shut, and stood in the midst, and said: Peace be to you.

"Then He saith to Thomas: Put in thy finger hither, and see My hands; and bring hither thy hand, and put it into My side; and be not faithless, but believing.

"Thomas answered, and said to Him: My Lord, and my God.

"BRING HITHER THY HAND, AND PUT IT INTO MY SIDE"

IN JERUSALEM EIGHT DAYS LATER

"Jesus saith to him: Because thou hast seen Me, Thomas, thou hast believed: blessed are they that have not seen, and have believed." (St. John xx, 24–29.)

Although Thomas the Apostle at first showed himself distrustful, yet he was deeply and loyally attached to his Master, and we are eternally grateful to him for giving Our Lord the occasion to say: "Blessed are they that have not seen, and have believed."

QUESTIONS

1. At what times are we expected to use St. Thomas's words: "My Lord, and my God"?

2. Whom did Our Lord say were more blessed than St. Thomas?

3. What marks did St. Thomas and the other Apostles see in the Risen Body of Christ?

XXV

NEAR THE SEA OF GALILEE

THE SECOND DRAUGHT OF FISHES

The angel at the Resurrection had announced to
the holy women: "And going quickly, tell ye His
disciples that He is risen: and behold He will go
before you into Galilee; there you shall see Him."
(St. Matthew xxviii, 7.)

After the Passover season, many of the disciples
left Jerusalem and returned to their homes in Galilee. Shortly after their return to Capharnaum, seven
of their number went to the Sea of Tiberias. These
were Simon Peter, Thomas called Didymus, Nathanael of Cana in Galilee, the two sons of Zebedee,
and two others of His Apostles.

"Simon Peter saith to them: I go a fishing. They
say to him: We also come with thee." (St. John
xxii, 2–3.)

They pushed out their boats, and we can well
imagine what memories of bygone days came to
them as they sailed over the blue waters of the Sea.
Did they not recall the miraculous draught of fishes

"JESUS STOOD ON THE SHORE"

when Jesus had said to them: "Fear not: from henceforth thou shalt catch men"? (St. Luke v, 10.)

As on that former occasion, so now, the whole night passed but they caught nothing. And when morning came, "Jesus stood on the shore: yet the disciples knew not that it was Jesus.

"Jesus therefore said to them: Children, have you any meat? They answered Him: No.

"He saith to them: Cast the net on the right side of the ship, and you shall find." (St. John xxi, 4–6.)

The words caught the Apostles' attention, and the remembrance of another night on these same waters and at the same time made them cast in the net as directed. And the net was so loaded with fish that they were scarcely able to draw it up.

John alone, of all there, with his keen eye and loving heart, now recognized the Master and said to Peter: "It is the Lord." Simon Peter, when he heard that it was the Lord, girt his coat about him, and "cast himself into the sea."

"But the other disciples came in the ship, (for they were not far from the land, but as it were two hundred cubits,) dragging the net with fishes.

"As soon then as they came to land, they saw hot coals lying, and a fish laid thereon, and bread.

"Jesus said to them: Bring hither of the fishes which you have now caught.

NEAR THE SEA OF GALILEE

"Simon Peter went up, and drew the net to land, full of great fishes, one hundred and fifty-three. And although there were so many, the net was not broken.

"Jesus saith to them: Come, and dine. And none of them who were at meat, durst ask Him: Who art Thou? knowing that it was the Lord.

"And Jesus cometh and taketh bread, and giveth them, and fish in like manner.

"This is now the third time that Jesus was manifested to His disciples, after He was risen from the dead." (St. John xxi, 7–14.)

Once more the Apostles found themselves on the seashore at the Master's side, but no longer could they, on their part, feel the old free comradeship of bygone days, for "He was not of the world." The very sight of their Risen Lord overawed them, and so the morning meal was finished in silence.

QUESTIONS

1. Relate the story of the first draught of fishes. (See "The Journeys of Jesus, Book One," pp. 82–83.)

2. Compare the first draught with the second, as to persons, time, place, number of fishes caught, and circumstances.

3. Can you think of a reason why "none of them who were at meat, durst ask Him: Who art Thou?"

THE JOURNEYS OF JESUS

Peter is Made the Shepherd

"When therefore they had dined, Jesus saith to Simon Peter: Simon, son of John, lovest thou Me more than these? He saith to Him: Yea, Lord, Thou knowest that I love Thee. He saith to him: Feed My lambs.

"He saith to him again: Simon, son of John, lovest thou Me? He saith to Him: Yea, Lord, Thou knowest that I love Thee. He saith to him: Feed My lambs.

"He said to him the third time: Simon, son of John, lovest thou Me? Peter was grieved, because He had said to him the third time: Lovest thou Me? And he said to Him: Lord, Thou knowest all things: Thou knowest that I love Thee. He said to him: Feed My sheep.

"Amen, amen I say to thee, when thou wast younger, thou didst gird thyself, and didst walk where thou wouldst. But when thou shalt be old, thou shalt stretch forth thy hands, and another shall gird thee, and lead thee whither thou wouldst not.

"And this He said, signifying by what death he should glorify God. And when He had said this, He saith to him: Follow Me.

"Peter turning about, saw that disciple whom Jesus loved following, who also leaned on His breast at

[160]

supper, and said: Lord, who is he that shall betray Thee?

"Him therefore when Peter had seen, he saith to Jesus: Lord, and what shall this man do?

"Jesus saith to him: So I will have him to remain till I come, what is it to thee? follow thou Me.

"This saying therefore went abroad among the brethren, that that disciple should not die. And Jesus did not say to him: He should not die; but, So I will have him to remain till I come, what is it to thee?

"This is that disciple who giveth testimony of these things, and hath written these things; and we know that his testimony is true.

"But there are also many other things which Jesus did; which, if they were written every one, the world itself, I think, would not be able to contain the books that should be written." (St. John xxi, 15–25.)

QUESTIONS

1. Find the meaning of the word "primacy."

2. What is meant by the "Primacy of Peter"?

3. When, where, and in what circumstances was the Primacy given to Peter?

4. Locate on the map Cæsarea-Philippi.

5. Read what had happened at Cæsarea-Philippi. (See "The Journeys of Jesus, Book Two," pp. 28–30.)

THE JOURNEYS OF JESUS

JESUS REVEALS HIMSELF TO ELEVEN DISCIPLES

"And the eleven disciples went into Galilee, unto the mountain where Jesus had appointed them.

"And seeing Him they adored: but some doubted.

"And Jesus coming, spoke to them, saying: All power is given to Me in heaven and in earth.

"Going therefore, teach ye all nations; baptizing them in the Name of the Father, and of the Son, and of the Holy Ghost.

"Teaching them to observe all things whatsoever I have commanded you: and behold I am with you all days, even to the consummation of the world." (St. Matthew xxviii, 16–20.)

QUESTIONS

1. What commission did Jesus give to the eleven disciples on a mountain in Galilee?

2. Quote the words of Jesus on this occasion.

3. How is Christ with us "all days, even to the consummation of the world"?

XXVI

THE FORTY DAYS AFTER THE RESURRECTION

THE MANIFESTATIONS OF JESUS

In the Acts of the Apostles (i, 3) we are told that Jesus "showed Himself alive after His Passion, by many proofs, for forty days appearing to them, and speaking of the Kingdom of God."

We have seen (page 143) that the first appearance of Our Lord after His Resurrection was, in all probability, to His Blessed Mother. Though this appearance to His Mother is not recorded in the Gospels, it has been piously believed in the Church for many centuries.

The first recorded appearance of our Risen Lord is that in which He revealed Himself to Mary Magdalen; and the Gospels mention nine other manifestations. The recorded manifestations are as follows:

FIRST. To Mary Magdalen
SECOND. To the other women
THIRD. To St. Peter
FOURTH. To the two disciples on the way to Emmaus

[163]

THE JOURNEYS OF JESUS

FIFTH. To all the Apostles except St. Thomas, in the
Supper room
(These five appearances, and that to His Blessed
Mother, took place on Easter Sunday.)
SIXTH. To the Apostles, including St. Thomas, a week
later than Easter Sunday
SEVENTH. To seven Apostles near the Sea of Galilee
EIGHTH. To the Eleven, and to a multitude of disciples on
a mountain in Galilee
NINTH. To the Eleven "toward Bethania to the Mount of
Olives"
TENTH. To James, the son of Alpheus. (1 Cor. xv, 7)

QUESTIONS

1. In the New Testament find the recorded appearances of Jesus after His Resurrection.

2. Which appearance is not recorded, but is a pious
belief in the Church?

3. Which do you think is the greatest of all Christ's
miracles?

4. Which miracle is the foundation of our faith in
Christ?

THE ASCENSION INTO HEAVEN

"And He led them out as far as Bethania." (St.
Luke xxiv, 50.)
Our Saviour's earthly sojourn is ended, and now
He is ready to begin His glorious life in heaven.

Therefore He leads His disciples from Jerusalem toward the Mount of Olives.

On their way the disciples said to Jesus: "Lord, wilt Thou at this time restore again the kingdom to Israel?"

He told them that the time *when* and *how* it would be restored was in the Father's power. "But you shall receive the power of the Holy Ghost coming upon you, and you shall be witnesses unto Me in Jerusalem, and in all Judea, and Samaria, and even to the uttermost part of the earth."

And when He had said these things, lifting up His hands, He bestowed upon them a farewell blessing. While He blessed them, little by little His Sacred Body by His own power was raised up till It was hidden by a cloud.

"And a cloud received Him out of their sight," says the inspired writer of the Acts. While they stood transfixed in wonder and adoration, two angels in white garments appeared and said: "Ye men of Galilee, why stand you looking up to heaven? This Jesus Who is taken up from you into heaven, shall so come, as you have seen Him going into heaven." (Acts i, 6–11.)

These words of the angels must have reminded the Apostles of Our Lord's promise to them that He would not leave them orphans but would send the

Paraclete, the Comforter, to them. Then "they ador-
ing went back into Jerusalem with great joy.

"And they were always in the Temple, praising
and blessing God." (St. Luke xxiv, 52–53.)

QUESTIONS

1. Name two important events of Our Lord's life that
took place on Mount Olivet.

2. Describe the Saviour's ascension into heaven, as
recorded in St. Luke's Gospel, and as recorded in the Acts
of the Apostles.

XXVII

THE DAYS AFTER THE ASCENSION

Matthias Chosen to Take the Place of Judas

With the suicide of the traitor Judas, a vacancy was left in the number of the Twelve Apostles, and this gap in their ranks the remaining eleven took occasion to fill after Our Lord had ascended into heaven.

While therefore they awaited the coming of the Holy Ghost, Whom Christ had promised, St. Peter arose one day and declared that they must now choose some one of the many faithful ones who had followed Our Lord from the first of His public life to fill the place of Judas.

"Wherefore of these men who have companied with us all the time that the Lord Jesus came in and went out among us,

"Beginning from the Baptism of John, until the day wherein He was taken up from us, one of these must be made a witness with us of His Resurrection.

"And they appointed two, Joseph, called Barsabas, who was surnamed Justus, and Matthias.

THE JOURNEYS OF JESUS

"And praying, they said: Thou, Lord, Who knowest the hearts of all men, show whether of these two Thou hast chosen,

"To take the place of this ministry and apostleship, from which Judas hath by transgression fallen, that he might go to his own place.

"And they gave them lots, and the lot fell upon Matthias, and he was numbered with the eleven Apostles." (Acts i, 15–26.)

In this election we see St. Peter acting as head of the assembly, and the others submitting to his orders and directions.

QUESTIONS

1. Between the time of the Ascension of Christ and the time of the Descent of the Holy Ghost, what action of St. Peter showed that he was the Chief of the Apostles?

2. Who took the place left vacant by the traitor Judas?

3. What devout practice of the Church seems to date its beginning from this time?

The Descent of the Holy Ghost

The tenth day after the Ascension was the day on which the Jews celebrated the Feast of Pentecost, one of their three great, joyous feasts in thanksgiving to the Lord for the giving of the Law to Moses on Mount Sinai.

[168]

THE DAYS AFTER THE ASCENSION

And when the days of the Pentecost were accomplished, the Apostles were "all together in one place:

"And suddenly there came a sound from heaven, as of a mighty wind coming, and it filled the whole house where they were sitting.

"And there appeared to them parted tongues as it were of fire, and it sat upon every one of them:

"And they were all filled with the Holy Ghost, and they began to speak with divers tongues, according as the Holy Ghost gave them to speak." (Acts ii, 1–4.)

QUESTIONS

1. How many days were there between the Ascension of Christ and the Descent of the Holy Ghost?

2. Relate the manner of the coming of the Holy Ghost on the first Pentecost Sunday.

PETER'S FIRST SERMON

"Now there were dwelling at Jerusalem, Jews, devout men, out of every nation under heaven.

"And when this was noised abroad, the multitude came together, and were confounded in mind, because that every man heard them speak in his own tongue.

"And they were all amazed, and wondered, saying: Behold, are not all these, that speak, Galileans?

"And how have we heard, every man our own tongue wherein we were born? . . . we have heard them speak in our own tongues the wonderful works of God.

"And they were all astonished, and wondered, saying one to another: What meaneth this?

"But others mocking, said: These men are full of new wine.

"But Peter standing up with the Eleven, lifted up his voice, and spoke to them: Ye men of Judea, and all you that dwell in Jerusalem, be this known to you, and with your ears receive my words."

St. Peter then repeated to all present the words of the Prophets Joel and David foretelling the very thing which they were then witnessing. "For," said St. Peter, "these are not drunk, as you suppose, seeing it is but the third hour of the day. . . .

"Ye men of Israel, hear these words: Jesus of Nazareth, a Man approved of God among you, by miracles, and wonders, and signs, which God did by Him, in the midst of you, as you also know:

"This Same being delivered up, by the determinate counsel and foreknowledge of God, you by the hands of wicked men have crucified and slain. . . .

"This Jesus hath God raised again, whereof all we are witnesses."

Much more did Peter say to the multitude of the

things that the prophets had foretold of Christ. When they had heard these things, their hearts were filled with sorrow, and they "said to Peter, and to the rest of the Apostles: What shall we do, men and brethren?

"But Peter said to them: Do penance, and be baptized every one of you in the Name of Jesus Christ, for the remission of your sins: and you shall receive the gift of the Holy Ghost.

"For the promise is to you, and to your children, and to all that are far off, whomsoever the Lord our God shall call.

"And with very many other words did he testify and exhort them, saying: Save yourselves from this perverse generation.

"They therefore that received his word, were baptized; and there were added in that day about three thousand souls.

"And they were persevering in the doctrine of the Apostles, and in the communication of the breaking of bread, and in prayers.

"And fear came upon every soul: many wonders also and signs were done by the Apostles in Jerusalem, and there was great fear in all.

"And all they that believed, were together, and had all things common.

"Their possessions and goods they sold, and divided them to all, according as every one had need.

THE JOURNEYS OF JESUS

"And continuing daily with one accord in the Temple, and breaking bread from house to house, they took their meat with gladness and simplicity of heart;

"Praising God, and having favor with all the people. And the Lord increased daily together such as should be saved." (Acts ii, 5–47.)

QUESTIONS

1. How many were converted by St. Peter's first sermon?

2. How did it happen that so many people were in Jerusalem on that day?

3. What was particularly noteworthy in his sermon?

4. What gave St. Peter and the other Apostles such fearless courage?

5. What can you say of the charity of the early converts?

6. What daily act of piety did they practice?

7. Give in your own words the meaning of these words: "And the Lord increased daily together such as should be saved."

THE BIRTHDAY OF THE CHURCH

The Descent of the Holy Ghost on the First Pentecost is, then, the real birthday of the Church. It was the day when there was complete fulfilment of the mission of our Blessed Lord. From His home in Nazareth He had gone forth, as we have seen, and had journeyed to and fro among the people, teaching them, working miracles, and laying the foundations of the Church which was to continue His work after He had gone to heaven. Now with the Church founded, and the Apostles confirmed, the last great journey of Our Lord was at an end.

BIBLICAL GLOSSARY

KEY. făt, fāte, ärm, sofạ, mĕt, mēte, ênough, hẽr, novẹl, ĭt, īce, nŏt, nōte, melọn, fŏŏt, fōōd, ŭp, ūse, ûrn, stirrụp.

Andrew (ăn'drōō) : one of the twelve Apostles, and the brother of Peter.

Annas (ăn'ạs) : the father-in-law of Caiphas, and at one time the high priest.

Ascension (ạ sĕn'shụn) : Christ's ascending into heaven in the presence of His Apostles.

Azymès, Feast of (ăz'ĭmz) : the feast of the unleavened bread among the Jews.

Barabbas (bạ răb'ạs) : a noted criminal, chosen by the Jews to be released in preference to Christ.

Bartholomew (bär thŏl'ô mū) : one of the Apostles, thought to be the same as Nathanael.

Bethania (bĕ thā'nĭ ạ), or **Bethany:** a village two miles from Jerusalem, on the eastern slope of Mount Olivet.

Bethphage (bĕth'fạ jē) : a village near Bethany.

Cæsar (sē'zạr) : the title of the Roman emperor.

Cæsar Augustus (ô gŭs'tụs) : emperor of Rome from 27 B.C. to 14 A.D.

Caiphas (kā'yạ fạs) : the high priest at the time of the Crucifixion. He was the son-in-law of Annas.

Calvary (kăl'vạ rĭ) : the place where Our Lord was crucified.

BIBLICAL GLOSSARY

Cedron (sē′drǫn), or **Kedron** (kē′drǫn) : the brook on the eastern side of the city of Jerusalem.

Cenacle (sĕn′ạ k′l) : the room in which the Last Supper was eaten.

Cleophas (klē′ô făs) : supposed to be the same as Alpheus.

Corbona (kǒr bō′nạ) : the treasury or alms-box to which the Jewish people contributed for the upkeep of the Temple and its ceremonies of worship.

Dismas (dĭs′măs) : supposed to be the name of the thief who repented on the cross.

Emmaus (ĕ mā′ŭs) : the town where Christ made Himself known to two of His disciples after His Resurrection.

Eucharist (ū′kạ rĭst) : the Sacrament of the Body and Blood of Christ.

Evangelist (ĕ văn′jĕl ĭst) : a word used to describe those who wrote the Gospels. St. John, the writer of the fourth Gospel, is called "the Evangelist" to distinguish him from St. John the Baptist.

Galilee (găl′ĭ lē) : the most northern of the provinces of Palestine at the time of Christ.

Galilee, Sea of: a lake named from the province of Galilee, twelve or fourteen miles long and six or seven miles wide. Called also Sea of Chinnereth, Lake of Genesareth, and Sea of Tiberias.

Gesmas (gĕs′măs) : thought to be the name of the impenitent thief.

Gethsemani (gĕth sĕm′ạ nĕ) : a garden across the Brook of Cedron, at the foot of Mount Olivet, which was the scene of Christ's agony and bloody sweat.

Golgotha (gŏl′gô thạ) : the Hebrew name for the place where Christ was crucified.

[176]

BIBLICAL GLOSSARY

Haceldama (hạ sĕl'dạ mạ) **(The Field of Blood):** the name of the potter's field (a burying place for strangers) which was purchased with the thirty pieces of silver that Judas returned to the Jewish priests, after he had betrayed Christ.

Hebrews (hē'brōōz) : the name given to all the descendants of Jacob. They were also called Israelites and Jews.

Herodians (hĕ rō'dĭ ạnz) : the members of a political party of Jews whose special aim was to promote Herod's interests, and who in consequence acknowledged Roman laws.

Hosanna (hǒ zăn'ạ) : the joyful cry of the Jews when they greeted Christ entering Jerusalem in triumph.

James (jāmz) : one of the three favorite Apostles, the brother of John and the son of Zebedee.

James the Lesser: one of the Apostles, the son of Alpheus and Mary.

Jeremias (jĕr ê mī'ạs) : one of the four great prophets.

Jerusalem (jĕ rōō'sạ lĕm) : the capital of Palestine, thirty-two miles from the Mediterranean and eighteen miles from the river Jordan. The sacred city of the Jewish people.

John: the beloved disciple, son of Zebedee, and brother of James.

Jordan (jôr'dạn) : the only river in Palestine, rising in Mount Hermon and emptying into the Dead Sea.

Joseph of Arimathea (ăr ĭ mạ thē'ạ) : a wealthy man, a member of the Sanhedrin, who became a disciple of Christ.

Judas (jōō'dạs), or **Thaddeus** (thăd'dĕ ụs) : one of the Apostles, a brother of James the Lesser; also called Jude.

Judas Iscariot (ĭs kăr'ĭ ǫt) : one of the twelve Apostles, the one who betrayed Christ.

Malchus (măl'kụs) : the high priest's servant whose ear was cut off by Peter in the garden when Jesus was captured.

[177]

BIBLICAL GLOSSARY

Mary Magdalen (măg'dạ lĕn): a sinful woman who was converted by Christ, and who became one of the great saints of the Church.

Matthew (măth'ū): one of the twelve Apostles, the writer of the first Gospel; also known as Levi.

Matthias (mạ thī'ăs): the one chosen by lot to take the place of Judas as one of the twelve Apostles.

Nazarenes (năz ạ rēnz'): residents of Nazareth; also applied to the followers of Jesus.

Nicodemus (nĭk ô dē'mụs): the Jewish admirer of Jesus who came to see Our Saviour by night. He was a member of the Sanhedrin, but he took no part in the condemnation of Christ. He was among those who took the Body of Christ down from the Cross and laid it in the tomb.

Olivet (ŏl'ĭ vĕt), **Mount:** a noted mountain east of Jerusalem; the Mount of the Ascension.

Paraclete (păr'ạ klēt): the Comforter, the Holy Ghost.

Parasceve (păr'ạ sēv): the eve of the Jewish Sabbath. In this book it refers to the day on which Christ was crucified.

Pasch (păsk): the feast of the Passover among the Jews, a term later applied to Easter.

Passover (păs'ō vēr), **Feast of the:** the principal feast of the Jews, reminding them of the sparing of the families of the Israelites when the destroying angel killed the first-born of Egypt.

Pentecost (pĕn'tĕ kŏst), **Feast of:** a great feast among the Jews fifty days after the Passover, called the Feast of Weeks. Also the day of the Descent of the Holy Ghost upon the Apostles, now a feast celebrated by the Catholic Church seven weeks after Easter.

Pharisees (făr'ĭ sēz): a religious sect among the Jews.

BIBLICAL GLOSSARY

Philip (fĭl′ĭp) : an Apostle whose home was in Bethsaida.

Phylacteries (fĭ lăk′tēr ĭz) : little leathern boxes containing strips of parchment on which were written certain passages from the Scripture. Two of these, one fastened on the head and the other on the left arm, were worn by Jews at morning prayer. The Pharisees wore them broader than the rest of the people.

Pontius Pilate (pŏn′shĭ ŭs pī′lăt) : the sixth Roman governor of Judea, before whom Christ was tried.

Primacy (prī′mạ sĭ) : it here refers to St. Peter as the first principal or supreme bishop of the Christian Church.

Sadducees (săd′û sēz) : a religious sect among the Jews.

Sanhedrin (săn′hĕ drĭn) : the great council of the Jews.

Simon of Cyrene (sī rē′nē) : the man who was compelled by the executioners of Our Lord to help Him bear His Cross.

Simon Peter (sī′mọn pē′tēr) : the chief of the Apostles, whose name was Simon, afterwards changed to Peter.

Simon Zelotes (zĕ lō′tēz) : one of the twelve Apostles. He is called Zelotes (or the Zealot) to distinguish him from St. Peter, whose name was originally Simon.

Sinai (sī′nī) : the mountain on which Moses received the Ten Commandments.

Temple (tĕm′p'l) : the chief place of worship among the Jews, built upon Mount Moriah in Jerusalem.

Thomas (tŏm′ạs) : one of the twelve Apostles; also called Didymus.

www.ingramcontent.com/pod-product-compliance
Lightning Source LLC
LaVergne TN
LVHW011229080426
835509LV00005B/403